2ND EDITION REVISED & EXPANDED

D1427805

CLUES FROM THE BIDDING
at bridge

MASTER POINT PRESS | TORONTO

Master Point Press
331 Douglas Ave.
Toronto, Ontario, Canada
M5M 1H2
(416) 781-0351
Website: http://www.masterpointpress.com
Email: info@masterpointpress.com

Library and Archives Canada Cataloguing in Publication

Pottage, Julian
        Clues from the bidding at bridge / written by Julian Pottage.

ISBN 1-894154-96-7

1. Contract bridge--Bidding.   I. Title.

GV1282.4.P65 2005   795.41'52   C2005-905198-1

Editor	Ray Lee
Cover and interior design	Olena S. Sullivan/New Mediatrix
Interior format	Luise Lee
Copyediting	Suzanne Hocking

Printed in Canada by Webcom Ltd.

1 2 3 4 5 6 7   09 08 07 06 05

Introduction

Defenders invariably base their strategy on declarer's bidding. Yet so often declarers fail to return the compliment, bashing on without a thought of what the defenders have or have not done.

Just one bid from a defender may tip you off to the winning play — perhaps warning of a bad break or that a finesse is doomed. When the defenders have made several bids you may be able to make spectacular double-dummy plays.

A corollary is that it is advisable to enter the auction only if (i) a genuine chance exists that your side will secure the contract, or (ii) your action might well stop the opponents from reaching their right contract or (iii) doing so will help partner in the play or with the opening lead. Players who bid on a weak hand without first weighing up the pros and cons are asking for trouble.

The bidding in this book generally assumes a UK rubber-bridge style with a variable notrump, theoretically with four-card major openings. For the benefit of readers unfamiliar with these methods, I have given the range for each 1NT opening as it occurs and explained anything out of the ordinary.

As you read the book, you may find that your ability to draw inferences from the opponents' bidding — or non-bidding — gets sharper. However, as the majority of the more difficult problems come in the second half, do not feel disappointed if your tally of correct answers fails to improve noticeably.

May I say that you will be missing an opportunity if you only take enough time to form a rough idea of what you would like to do before turning the page. You will learn more (and, just as important, get more answers right) if you study each deal conscientiously and form a detailed plan.

Julian Pottage 2005

Acknowledgments

The author is especially indebted to Terence Reese for his help in drafting the original edition of this book. Peter Crawley and Hugh Kelsey also performed a valuable editing role.

The author also owes his gratitude to William Bailey, Peter Burrows, Maureen Dennison, Ron Garber and Ray Lee for enabling this expanded and improved edition to appear in print.

Contents

Defensive Points

```
        ♠ 10 5
        ♡ J 10 6
        ◇ A 7 3
        ♣ A Q 10 7 6

                N
♠6 led      W       E
                S

        ♠ Q 8 2
        ♡ A Q 9 8 3 2
        ◇ K 9 6 4
        ♣ —
```

Dealer West
Both vul.

WEST	NORTH	EAST	SOUTH
2♠¹	pass	pass	3♡
pass	4♡	all pass	

1. Weak.

West leads a presumably fourth-best ♠6 and East wins the first trick with the ♠A before returning the nine. West wins with the jack and continues with the king. What do you play from dummy?

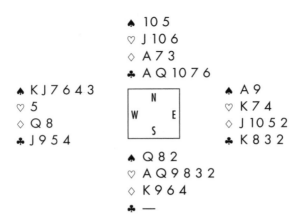

```
              ♠ 10 5
              ♡ J 10 6
              ◇ A 7 3
              ♣ A Q 10 7 6
♠ K J 7 6 4 3      N        ♠ A 9
♡ 5           W        E     ♡ K 7 4
◇ Q 8              S        ◇ J 10 5 2
♣ J 9 5 4                  ♣ K 8 3 2
              ♠ Q 8 2
              ♡ A Q 9 8 3 2
              ◇ K 9 6 4
              ♣ —
```

You are playing in 4♡. In view of West's vulnerable weak two opening you can feel fairly confident that the spades are 6-2. The danger of ruffing the third round of spades with the jack of hearts is that East may overruff with the king, leaving you with an almost certain diamond loser.

There can be no overruff if West has the king of hearts, but that would not help you very much anyway. Unless it was a singleton, you would lose a trump and a diamond.

On the third spade, you should discard a diamond from dummy, planning later to ruff a diamond. Naturally, you will draw two rounds of trumps, finessing East for the king, before taking the diamond ruff (in case West holds a 6-2-1-4 shape).

An interesting defensive point arises if declarer mistakenly ruffs the third spade in dummy. After overruffing with the king, East must return a diamond to break up the impending simple squeeze in the minors.

A different instructive point would arise if you correctly threw a diamond from dummy on the third spade but East held a club more and a diamond fewer than shown in the diagram. In that case, that defender could discard a diamond and later overruff the third round of diamonds.

Stop in Time

```
              ♠ 8 7 6 3
              ♡ J 7
              ♦ A 5 3
              ♣ A Q 10 8

                  ┌─────────┐
                  │    N    │
   ♠ J led        │ W     E │
                  │    S    │
                  └─────────┘

              ♠ A 5
              ♡ A K 4
              ♦ Q 8 4 2
              ♣ K J 7 2
```

Dealer South
E–W vul.

WEST	NORTH	EAST	SOUTH
			1♣
1♠	3♣	pass	3NT
all pass			

You are playing a weak notrump at this vulnerability; in your methods the 1♣ opening guarantees a club suit. Partner might have cuebid 2♠ (the standard way to show a raise based on high-card values in competition play), but the partnership would surely have reached the same final contract.

West leads the jack of spades (consistent with a suit headed by the K-J-10) and East follows with the two. How do you intend to play?

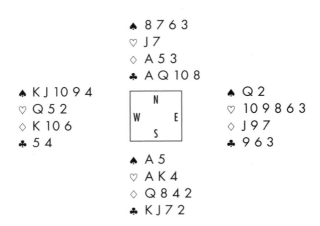

Nobody would overcall 1♠ on a moderate four-card suit and at most 10 points, which means that losing the lead is very likely to prove fatal to your 3NT contract. Indeed West does not have much for a vulnerable overcall, even with a five-card suit, if East has either the heart queen or the diamond king.

You have eight tricks on top and need one more. You might hold up the ♠A and try running the diamond eight, hoping that West will not gain the lead. This works if East's diamonds include the J-10-9 or, less likely, the king.

However, in light of the bidding and the vulnerability, an endplay on West offers the best shot. Win the second round of spades, cash two high clubs, the king and ace, and then exit with a spade.

On the long spades, you can discard two diamonds and a club from hand and one diamond from dummy. Having run out of clubs, West must now lead into a red-suit tenace.

The trap you must avoid is taking a third round of clubs, thinking to improve your chance of stripping West's exit cards. This would leave you with no discard on the fifth spade: if you let go your last club, West could block the hearts by leading the queen. True, you could play three clubs and two hearts, playing West to be 5-2-3-3, but a 3-5 heart split is more likely than 2-6.

Ominous Opening

```
        ♠ K Q J 3
        ♡ 7 5 4
        ◇ K 5 4
        ♣ K Q 10

              N
  ♡ 6 led   W     E
              S

        ♠ 10 7 5
        ♡ A J 10
        ◇ Q J 6 3
        ♣ A J 7
```

Dealer West
Both vul.

WEST	NORTH	EAST	SOUTH
1♡	1♠	pass	2NT
pass	3NT	all pass	

With values for an opening bid and a chunky K-Q-J at the top, one cannot fault North's overcall on a four-card suit. If the option had been available, you might have made a cuebid of 2♡ to indicate fair values and spade support.

West leads the six of hearts and East plays the queen. What plan should you make on this one?

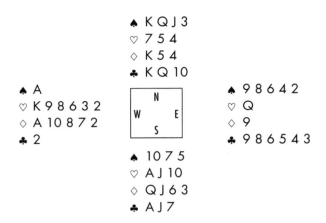

```
              ♠ K Q J 3
              ♡ 7 5 4
              ◇ K 5 4
              ♣ K Q 10
♠ A                              ♠ 9 8 6 4 2
♡ K 9 8 6 3 2      N             ♡ Q
◇ A 10 8 7 2    W     E          ◇ 9
♣ 2                S             ♣ 9 8 6 5 4 3
              ♠ 10 7 5
              ♡ A J 10
              ◇ Q J 6 3
              ♣ A J 7
```

The opening bid of 1♡ on your left is ominous. West must have both of the missing aces, which will be entries to establish and run the hearts.

By far your best chance to make your 3NT contract on the heart lead is to hope that East's queen of hearts is a singleton. Therefore, duck the first trick. With a little care, you should have time to establish three spade tricks and two diamond tricks.

If East returns a club, win with the ace and lead a spade. If West ducks two spades (not that this can happen as the cards lie), you can play a diamond to the king and then revert to spades.

Note that refusing to win with A-J-10 might sometimes work well if the leader's partner holds all the entries:

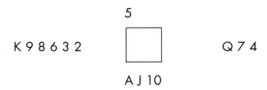

```
                    5
K 9 8 6 3 2       [   ]        Q 7 4
                  A J 10
```

If you expect East to get in twice, allowing the queen to win the first round might mean that you lose two tricks in the suit instead of four.

Timely Concession

```
        ♠ K 9 6 5
        ♡ K 9 3 2
        ◇ 6 4
        ♣ K 8 2
```

```
              N
◇ K led    W     E
              S
```

```
        ♠ A Q J 10 8 2
        ♡ 10 5
        ◇ A 5
        ♣ A 9 5
```

Dealer South
Neither vul.

WEST	NORTH	EAST	SOUTH
			1♠
2NT	3♠	pass	4♠
all pass			

West's 2NT, obviously, is the Unusual Notrump, denoting a minor two-suiter. The suggestion I made in the introduction about weighing up the pros and cons of any intervention applies particularly to descriptive bids like an Unusual 2NT. The ability to offer partner a choice of two suits in which to play, thereby increasing the chance of buying the contract, certainly counts as a plus, but a good player would consider the negatives as well.

West leads the king of diamonds. How will you tackle the play?

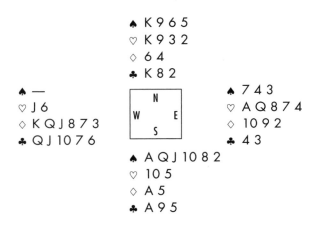

♠ K 9 6 5
♡ K 9 3 2
◇ 6 4
♣ K 8 2

♠ —
♡ J 6
◇ K Q J 8 7 3
♣ Q J 10 7 6

♠ 7 4 3
♡ A Q 8 7 4
◇ 10 9 2
♣ 4 3

♠ A Q J 10 8 2
♡ 10 5
◇ A 5
♣ A 9 5

You are playing in 4♠ on a diamond lead after West has made an
Unusual Notrump. Since East must have more hearts than West,
the ace of hearts may well sit over the king, which means you
might lose two tricks in hearts and one in each of the minors.
Fortunately, you can turn to your advantage the knowledge that
East will have at most a doubleton in clubs.

Start by taking the diamond king with the ace and drawing
trumps. After that, concede a diamond to cut the defenders'
communications. West cannot lead a heart without giving you a
trick, and you can win the club return in dummy with the king,
cross to the ace of clubs and lead a heart, covering West's card.
East is endplayed and forced to establish a heart trick for the
dummy (or give a ruff and discard, which suits you just as well).

Did you think it could do no harm to duck the first diamond?
It might if West had a small singleton in each major and East
cleverly won West's heart switch with the jack and returned a
small heart.

As the cards lie, and assuming that you find the winning line,
the opponents would have done better to sacrifice in 5◇ doubled,
losing only 100. However, with no values in the minors and poor
shape, I do not think you can blame East for passing over 3♠, and
West could hardly bid again.

Parking Place

```
        ♠ A 8
        ♡ 10 9 5 4 3
        ◇ J 8 7
        ♣ A K 10
```

♡K led

```
        N
    W       E
        S
```

```
        ♠ K Q J 10 5 4 3
        ♡ A
        ◇ K 5
        ♣ Q 6 4
```

Dealer South
Both vul.

WEST	NORTH	EAST	SOUTH
			1♠
dbl	redbl	pass	pass[1]
2◇	pass	pass	4♠
pass	5♣[2]	pass	6♠
all pass			

1. Implying a non-minimum opening.
2. Cuebid agreeing spades.

Reaching a slam after an opposing takeout double does not happen every day. How do you think you can land the contract after the king of hearts is led?

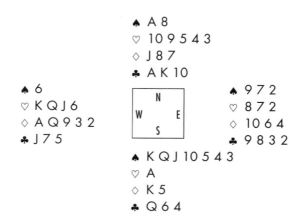

♠ A 8
♥ 10 9 5 4 3
♦ J 8 7
♣ A K 10

♠ 6
♥ K Q J 6
♦ A Q 9 3 2
♣ J 7 5

N
W E
S

♠ 9 7 2
♥ 8 7 2
♦ 10 6 4
♣ 9 8 3 2

♠ K Q J 10 5 4 3
♥ A
♦ K 5
♣ Q 6 4

The bidding marks West, who made a takeout double, with the ace of diamonds. So, to make your contract of 6♠, you will need to find a parking place for your diamond loser. You will have chances if hearts break 4-3, which seems almost a certainty, as someone with a five-card heart suit would surely have bid the suit over 1♠ redoubled.

A little calculation will establish that you may find yourself an entry short to set up and cash the long heart. Two possibilities present themselves for finding an extra entry: you can play West for the nine of spades or for the jack of clubs. As West figures to be short in spades and have support (or at least tolerance) for clubs, the clubs represent much the better chance.

Having won the heart lead perforce, take the king and ace of spades, ruff a heart and draw the last trump. Be careful, now, to lead the *queen* of clubs and overtake. A later finesse of the ♣10 will create the entry you need. If you mistakenly begin with a club to the ace, West may spike your guns on the second round of the suit by inserting the jack. You will then succeed only in the unlikely event that the queen and jack of hearts come down in the next two rounds of hearts.

Wise Withdrawal

```
        ♠ J 7 3 2
        ♡ K Q 9
        ◇ A K J 8 3
        ♣ Q
```

♣J led

```
        N
    W       E
        S
```

```
        ♠ A K Q 9
        ♡ A 8
        ◇ 5 4 2
        ♣ K 7 4 3
```

Dealer South
Both vul.

WEST	NORTH	EAST	SOUTH
			1NT
pass	2♣	pass	2♠
pass	3◇	pass	3NT
pass	5♠	pass	6♠
pass	pass	dbl	6NT
all pass			

Over your strong notrump, a Stayman inquiry quickly located the 4-4 fit and North's 3◇ was forcing. His 5♠ on the next round invited you to bid a slam and expressed doubt about the trump situation.

East wins the jack of clubs lead with the ace and you get in on the second round of clubs. How will you play for twelve tricks? (Remember that East doubled 6♠ and that you are now in 6NT.)

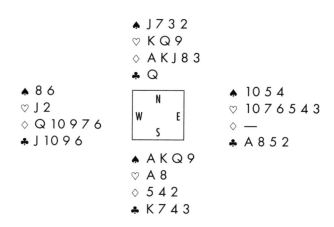

In 6NT, you need four diamond tricks to add to the eight you have in the other suits. Ordinarily you would cash the ace first and, depending upon whether East dropped the nine or higher or whether only small cards appeared, you would look to finesse the eight or the jack on the second round. Obviously East's double of 6♠ provides the clue here. It is not too difficult to work out that this was a request for a diamond lead, based on a void in the suit and the expectation of a ruff.

Having come this far, you must not relax too soon. You must take care not to play too many rounds of spades early on. The original declarer foolishly cashed all the spades before leading a round of diamonds. Unfortunately, West went in with the ◇9 on the first round of the suit and the ◇10 on the second. The declarer had to concede a diamond at the finish.

As you can see, you did the right thing in retreating from 6♠ doubled, but what do you think of East's double? It was risky for several reasons. For one, West might find the diamond lead anyway; for another, 6♠ might prove awkward with the hostile diamond break whatever the lead; finally, as you had both opened with 1NT and bid 3NT later, East might have foreseen the flight to 6NT.

Guess the Minors

```
        ♠ J 9 7
        ♡ K 5
        ◇ J 10 6 5
        ♣ J 10 7 5
```

```
        N
    W       E
        S
```

♠ 3 led

```
        ♠ A
        ♡ A Q J 10 9 7 4
        ◇ Q 9 3
        ♣ K 6
```

Dealer East
E–W vul.

WEST	NORTH	EAST	SOUTH
		pass	1 ♡
pass	1NT	pass	4 ♡
all pass			

With 6-point hands, you should invariably respond if partner opens at the one-level and you are not playing a strong club system. Although the 4-3-2-1 count tends to overvalue jacks (and queens), North's 1NT response seems fine with the king in partner's suit and the jacks all supported by intermediate cards.

West leads the three of spades. East covers the nine with the ten and your ace wins. The contract looks likely to depend on making a club trick. What are your thoughts on the matter?

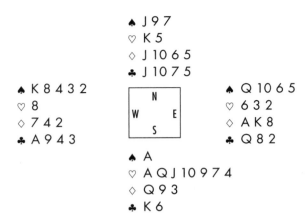

♠ J 9 7
♡ K 5
◇ J 10 6 5
♣ J 10 7 5

♠ K 8 4 3 2
♡ 8
◇ 7 4 2
♣ A 9 4 3

♠ Q 10 6 5
♡ 6 3 2
◇ A K 8
♣ Q 8 2

♠ A
♡ A Q J 10 9 7 4
◇ Q 9 3
♣ K 6

You play in 4♡ having opened 1♡ in second seat. West leads the three of spades to the nine, ten and ace.

The play to the first trick marks the ♠Q-10 or ♠K-10 on your right and the king or queen on your left. More importantly, it suggests that West does not hold the ◇A-K, as that would have been an attractive combination from which to lead.

The defenders have not made a positive bid, but East's initial pass could be significant. If the ace and king of diamonds lie in opposite hands, anyone could hold the club ace. However, if East has both the ace and king of diamonds, West must hold the ace, as East would not have passed with 13 or 14 points.

You lack the entries to do any significant testing, so your best plan is to take two rounds of trumps ending in dummy, and then *run* the club jack. You should do it that way because East may hold the ◇A-K, in which case West must hold the ace of clubs.

It would be weak play to draw the trumps and then attempt to gain entry to the table in diamonds. It should not prove too difficult for the opponents to play their stoppers at the right moment.

Playing as suggested, you may be leaving a trump out when you run the club jack. However, even if the diamonds split 4-2 and the trumps 3-1, the defenders may not find their ruff.

Weak Heart

```
        ♠ 5 4
        ♡ 9 6 3 2
        ◇ 10 6 5
        ♣ J 8 7 3
```

♡ K led

```
      ┌─────────┐
      │    N    │
      │ W     E │
      │    S    │
      └─────────┘
```

```
        ♠ K Q J 10 8 2
        ♡ —
        ◇ Q J 3
        ♣ A K Q 9
```

Dealer East
Both vul.

WEST	NORTH	EAST	SOUTH
		2♡	dbl
3♡	pass	pass	4♠
all pass			

One of the opponents has again opened with a weak two-bid. Based on the fact that they stopped in 3♡, you feel entitled to hope for at least one useful card opposite, but your partner's contribution seems modest.

You ruff the opening heart lead and note that you may have some problem in retaining trump control. How will you set about the play?

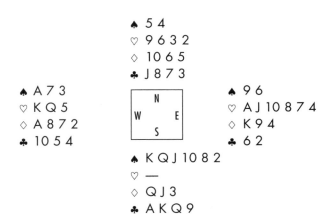

```
                ♠ 5 4
                ♡ 9 6 3 2
                ◇ 10 6 5
                ♣ J 8 7 3
  ♠ A 7 3                        ♠ 9 6
  ♡ K Q 5          N             ♡ A J 10 8 7 4
  ◇ A 8 7 2     W     E          ◇ K 9 4
  ♣ 10 5 4         S             ♣ 6 2
                ♠ K Q J 10 8 2
                ♡ —
                ◇ Q J 3
                ♣ A K Q 9
```

You have only three top losers in 4♠ but, after the heart lead, there is going to be a problem retaining control.

Suppose you start with a sly ten of spades. A smart West will go straight in with the ace and lead a second heart. You can ruff and draw trumps, but now you find yourself a tempo behind. West, still in good form, will capture the first diamond and force you again with a third round of hearts. This takes your last trump, so East will make a diamond and a heart at the finish.

You must play diamonds first, taking advantage of the fact that East's weak two and West's raise make it almost certain that hearts are 3-6 and that East is twice as likely to hold a top diamond as the ♠A. Before doing anything else, lead the ◇3 from hand. Suppose West does well and goes in with the ace to lead another heart. You ruff and play another diamond. East wins and forces you again. The crucial difference is that West, upon getting in with the ♠A, will have no more hearts to play.

Admittedly, by following this sequence, you may run into a diamond ruff, but this might equally happen if you try to draw trumps before playing diamonds. There is also some danger of a club ruff, but if East wins the first diamond and leads a club, then you can switch to drawing trumps.

Good Recovery

```
          ♠ A J 8 3
          ♡ A 8 7 6
          ◇ 5 4
          ♣ A 6 5
```

◇ J led

```
      ┌─────────┐
      │    N    │
      │ W     E │
      │    S    │
      └─────────┘
```

```
          ♠ K 10 9 7 4 2
          ♡ K 4
          ◇ A K Q
          ♣ Q 7
```

Dealer West
E–W vul.

WEST	NORTH	EAST	SOUTH
pass	1NT[1]	pass	3♠
pass	4♣[2]	pass	4◇[2]
pass	4♡[2]	pass	5♠[3]
pass	6♠	all pass	

1. 12-14.
2. Cuebid.
3. Asking for good trumps.

Whatever you may think of the bidding, you have reached an excellent slam. West leads the diamond jack. How do you play to escape the hideous possibility of losing a spade and a club?

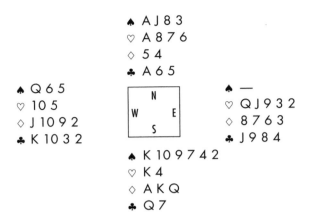

```
              ♠ A J 8 3
              ♡ A 8 7 6
              ◇ 5 4
              ♣ A 6 5
♠ Q 6 5          N          ♠ —
♡ 10 5      W        E      ♡ Q J 9 3 2
◇ J 10 9 2       S         ◇ 8 7 6 3
♣ K 10 3 2                 ♣ J 9 8 4
              ♠ K 10 9 7 4 2
              ♡ K 4
              ◇ A K Q
              ♣ Q 7
```

Your slam contract of 6♠ will be in danger only if trumps break 3-0 and you play the wrong top card first. In this case, you will probably need to find the defender holding three trumps with the king of clubs as well, giving you chances of a successful endplay.

You have no good clue to the trump situation, but there is a slight indication as to the position of the king of clubs: with this card — and particularly with a K-J holding — East might have doubled North's cuebid of 4♣. Players do that.

This reasoning makes it better than even money that West has the ♣K. You should therefore place East with the missing trumps. If you are wrong, as in the actual layout, you may still recover.

After winning the diamond lead, play a spade to the ace. East shows out, but you still have a good chance. Now you must decide which red suit to strip first. You have fewer diamonds than hearts and an opening lead from J-x would hardly be attractive. So, having cashed the king of spades, you take your two remaining diamond winners, discarding a heart from dummy. After that, play the king of hearts, the ace of hearts and ruff dummy's last heart. If West does not overruff, exit with a trump and hope for a club lead away from the king (or a ruff and discard).

Undercover Tricks

```
            ♠ 10 7 4
            ♡ K Q 5
            ◇ 9 5 4 3
            ♣ 9 7 5
```

♠Q led

```
        N
    W       E
        S
```

```
            ♠ A 6
            ♡ A J 10
            ◇ K Q J
            ♣ A K 10 3 2
```

Dealer West
Neither vul.

WEST	NORTH	EAST	SOUTH
2♠	pass	pass	dbl
pass	3◇	pass	3NT
all pass			

After West's weak two you were correct to double — a direct 3NT bid would indicate a strong desire to play there even if North had a bit of shape. Many pairs play that after the takeout double North bids 2NT on a worthless hand; your partnership had no such agreement.

West leads the queen of spades and East follows with the five. How do you plan to score nine tricks in time?

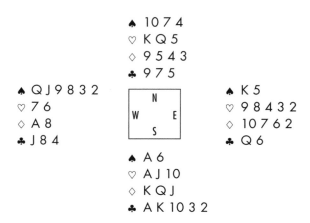

In view of the weak two opening, you can place West with six spades to the Q-J and East with a doubleton king. To make 3NT, you must start by blocking the spade suit by winning with the ace on the first round; you can then knock out the ace of diamonds.

At this point, you have eight tricks on top. If West leads a second spade and East exits in hearts, win in dummy and lead a club to the ace (unless East inserts the queen). Next, you cash the rest of the top diamonds and find that the suit does not break evenly. So, cross to the ♡K and lead a second club from the table. When the queen appears, let it hold. East can cash the ◇10, but you lose only one spade, two diamonds and a club.

Opportunities to block a suit appear in a variety of guises and are more frequent than you might think:

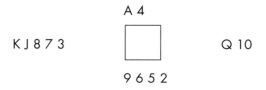

Since most defenders would lead a high card from holdings such as K-Q-10-x-x, K-J-10-x-x or Q-J-10-x-x, you should often play dummy's ace if West leads the seven.

Fast Run

```
        ♠ 9 6 3
        ♡ A K 7 3 2
        ◇ Q 10 3
        ♣ J 5
```

♠ 7 led

```
              N
          W       E
              S
```

```
        ♠ K 8
        ♡ Q
        ◇ A J 9 5 2
        ♣ A Q 10 6 3
```

Dealer North
Both vul.

WEST	NORTH	EAST	SOUTH
	pass	pass	1◇
1♠	2♡	pass	3♣
pass	3◇	pass	3NT
all pass			

West leads the seven of spades. East plays the jack and you have to win with the king. Presumably, the seven is fourth best from a five-card or longer spade suit headed by the A-Q-10-7. Consequently, a losing a finesse in one of the minors will result in defeat. How do you continue?

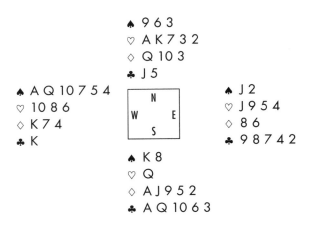

As both finesses go into the danger hand, even a 7-1 spade break will not help you make 3NT. Nor, if the suit splits 5-3, will cashing the ♡Q and playing a spade back in the hope of an endplay get you anywhere. You will have three discards to find and, at best, will end up forced to guess anyway. So, you must focus on trying to run nine tricks without losing the lead.

Five tricks in diamonds would see you home, but you must not ignore the chance of dropping a singleton king in one minor or the other before committing yourself to a finesse. Should you lay down the ace of clubs or the ace of diamonds?

On the basis that there are six clubs but only five diamonds missing, the king of diamonds is the more likely king to fall singleton under the ace. However, if you lay down the ace of diamonds unsuccessfully, the club finesse may bring you only three tricks. By contrast, you give yourself an extra chance if you start with the club ace. Even if the king does not fall, you can overtake the queen of hearts, cash the second heart, discarding a club, and play for five tricks in diamonds by running the queen. If the club king happens to drop, you will make one spade, *three* hearts (as the ♣J will give dummy an entry), one diamond and four clubs.

So, the ace of clubs has it.

neatly Done

```
        ♠ A 10 9 6 2
        ♡ 8 5
        ◇ A J 10
        ♣ A K Q
```

```
              N
♡ 6 led    W      E
              S
```

```
        ♠ Q
        ♡ A 9 7 4
        ◇ K 9 8 4 2
        ♣ J 10 8
```

Dealer North
N–S vul.

WEST	NORTH	EAST	SOUTH
	1♠	2♡	2NT
pass	3NT	all pass	

Some would make a negative double on the South cards, but how does this help if North, expecting to find support for both minors, rebids 3♣? Bidding 3NT over that would seem more of a stretch than the immediate 2NT response chosen.

West leads the six of hearts and East, who has bid hearts, plays the ten. Perhaps you will find the queen of diamonds and presumably make ten tricks … or perhaps not.

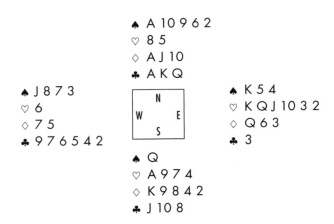

You are playing in 3NT after East has overcalled in hearts. West leads the six of hearts and East plays the ten, no doubt from K-Q-J-10-x or K-Q-J-10-x-x.

You have five winners outside diamonds — three clubs and the two major-suit aces. This means that, after holding up the ace of hearts, you can afford to lose a diamond — to West.

A snag could arise, however. Suppose you take the ace of hearts on the second round, cross to the ace of diamonds and lead the jack of diamonds. If East holds the queen of diamonds and covers, you will find the suit hopelessly blocked; obviously you cannot afford to duck and allow the defender with cashing hearts to win the trick.

There is an escape, though it's not easy to see at first. Since you are not afraid of a switch, win the *third* heart trick, discarding a *club* from dummy. Then cash the two club winners left in dummy and follow with ace and another diamond, intending to finesse. When East covers, you win and discard the blocking ten of diamonds on the jack of clubs. Rather neat, don't you think?

Tiny Error

♠ Q 10 3
♡ 10 7 5 4
◇ Q J 5
♣ A 10 7

```
      N
  W       E
      S
```

◇ A led

♠ A K J 9 8 7 2
♡ —
◇ 9 7 6
♣ K J 5

Dealer West
Both vul.

WEST	NORTH	EAST	SOUTH
1◇	pass	1♡	2♠
3♡	4♠	all pass	

At rubber bridge, your vulnerable jump overcall indicates quite a reasonable hand and North has no hesitation about bidding game, expecting it to make.

Indeed, when West leads a top diamond and dummy appears, you might envisage ten tricks — eleven if you get the clubs right. Alas, on the ◇A-K, East echoes with the ten and two. When West continues with the ◇8, East ruffs and then leads the queen of hearts. How do you plan to take the rest of the tricks? (You will find the remaining trumps 1-1.)

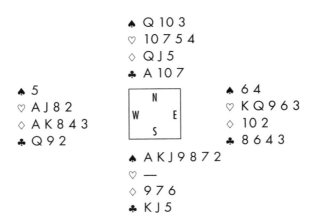

```
              ♠ Q 10 3
              ♡ 10 7 5 4
              ◇ Q J 5
              ♣ A 10 7
  ♠ 5                        ♠ 6 4
  ♡ A J 8 2       N          ♡ K Q 9 6 3
  ◇ A K 8 4 3   W   E        ◇ 10 2
  ♣ Q 9 2         S          ♣ 8 6 4 3
              ♠ A K J 9 8 7 2
              ♡ —
              ◇ 9 7 6
              ♣ K J 5
```

You play in 4♠ after West has opened 1◇ and raised East's hearts to the three-level. You lose the first three tricks — two top diamonds and a ruff — and all depends on finding the ♣Q for you to take the remainder.

What do you know about the distribution? The diamonds are 5-2 and no doubt the hearts are 4-5. A 2-1 trump break tells you, therefore, that West has three clubs to East's four. This suggests that East has the ♣Q. Moreover, if you believe the ♡Q, East needs to have the ♣Q, since with ace-king in both red suits and the ♣Q in a 1-4-5-3 shape, West would have bid four hearts, not three. Also, with only 3 points (the queen-jack of hearts), East might well have passed one diamond.

Thankfully, provided you do not squander the precious ♠2 on the first heart ruff, you have three trump entries to dummy. Use them to ruff three more hearts. When you find that East actually holds ♡K-Q-x-x-x, you might reasonably place West with the queen of clubs, although I admit this is no certainty.

Please note that East committed a tiny error in leading a heart after ruffing the third diamond. On a passive trump exit, declarer will lack the entries to ruff four rounds of hearts and may misjudge the position of the club queen.

Full of Grief

```
        ♠ K Q 4
        ♡ A K 6 5
        ◇ 9 6 2
        ♣ Q 5 4
```

```
            N
      W         E
            S
```

♠ J led

```
        ♠ 7 5 2
        ♡ Q 3
        ◇ A K 8
        ♣ K J 10 9 3
```

Dealer South
N–S vul.

WEST	NORTH	EAST	SOUTH
			1♣
pass	1♡	pass	1NT[1]
pass	3NT	all pass	

1. 12-14.

West leads the jack of spades — hardly a surprise since this is the unbid major.

3NT does not look difficult, but you need to think a little about your play, particularly to the first trick.

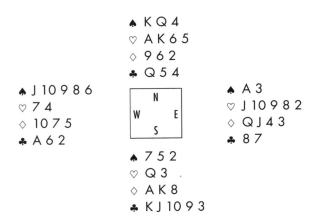

　　　　　　♠ K Q 4
　　　　　　♡ A K 6 5
　　　　　　◇ 9 6 2
　　　　　　♣ Q 5 4

♠ J 10 9 8 6　　　　　　　　♠ A 3
♡ 7 4　　　　　　　　　　　♡ J 10 9 8 2
◇ 10 7 5　　　　　　　　　　◇ Q J 4 3
♣ A 6 2　　　　　　　　　　♣ 8 7

　　　　　　♠ 7 5 2
　　　　　　♡ Q 3
　　　　　　◇ A K 8
　　　　　　♣ K J 10 9 3

After you have opened 1♣ and North has responded 1♡, you arrive in 3NT. When West leads the jack of spades you count your tricks: at least one in spades, three in hearts, two in diamonds and, after the ace has gone, four clubs — a total of at least ten. This means you need only focus on the danger of losing four spade tricks in addition to the club ace.

If dummy covers the jack of spades, you will go down if East has a doubleton ace of spades and West the ace of clubs. In practical terms, playing low from dummy will be fatal only if West has led from ♠A-J-10-x-x together with the ace of clubs. However, with a hand like that many people would have over-called with one spade, which makes this holding unlikely.

The possibility that West might hold a doubleton spade and the ace of clubs provides a further reason for playing low from dummy. Indeed, the original West held exactly that. Having seen the spade covered, East correctly played the ten from A-10-9-8-x to encourage a continuation and to maintain communications. Declarer was sorely disappointed when West later took the ace of clubs and played a second spade, allowing East to set the contract with four tricks in the suit.

No Optimist

```
        ♠ J 10 4 3
        ♡ A
        ◇ K 9 8 4
        ♣ K 7 6 4
```

```
            N
        W       E
            S
```

♡K led

```
        ♠ A K Q 6
        ♡ 8 7 5
        ◇ A 5
        ♣ A 8 3 2
```

Dealer West
Both vul.

WEST	NORTH	EAST	SOUTH
3♡	pass	pass	dbl
pass	4♡	pass	5♠
pass	6♠	all pass	

You had a tricky decision at your first turn. Although the shape suggested 3NT, the absence of a heart stopper did not. At your next turn, you reflect that you might have doubled with rather less than this, and that the hands appear to be fitting well, so you jump to 5♠. With a maximum for not having acted directly over 3♡, North happily accepts the invitation.

West leads the king of hearts against your slam. The play will present little challenge if both black suits break well, but life is rarely like that when an opponent has preempted.

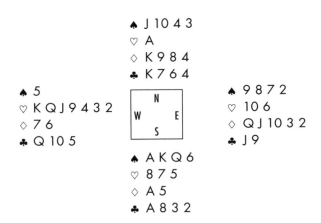

                    ♠ J 10 4 3
                    ♡ A
                    ◊ K 9 8 4
                    ♣ K 7 6 4
    ♠ 5   ♠ 9 8 7 2
    ♡ K Q J 9 4 3 2   ♡ 10 6
    ◊ 7 6   ◊ Q J 10 3 2
    ♣ Q 10 5   ♣ J 9
                    ♠ A K Q 6
                    ♡ 8 7 5
                    ◊ A 5
                    ♣ A 8 3 2

In 6♠, you have nine top tricks — four spades, one heart, two diamonds and two clubs. So, even counting two heart ruffs in
dummy, you need one more. If the clubs break 3-2, you can set
up another club trick. Still, you need to take care.

Suppose, after winning with the ace of hearts, you use the
two minor-suit aces as entries for ruffing two hearts (ruffing high
the second time). East will discard a club and you will need to
draw four rounds of trumps. Then, when you give up a club you
will find that West wins and has hearts to cash.

As the cards lie you could overcome this problem by cashing
the king of clubs earlier, but this would not work so well if East
had length in both minors: West might ruff your ace of clubs and
you would lose your squeeze chances.

The best way to avoid calamity is to begin by ducking a club.
True, you might go down at once if the clubs break 4-1, but you
are well placed otherwise. If West wins with a singleton queen
and switches to a trump, you can ruff two hearts in dummy and
one diamond in hand. You will then have to hope the last trump
squeezes East.

You might note that the play in 6♣ would be rather easier.
You would simply cash the ace-king of clubs and leave one
trump out. Of course, getting to 6♣ is another matter.

Time to Die

```
            ♠ A J 3 2
            ♡ K 10 5 4
            ◇ K 6 2
            ♣ 9 6
```

```
                 ┌─────────┐
                 │    N    │
♣7 led           │ W     E │
                 │    S    │
                 └─────────┘
```

```
            ♠ 10 7 5
            ♡ A Q J 9 6
            ◇ Q 8
            ♣ A J 5
```

Dealer East
N–S vul.

WEST	NORTH	EAST	SOUTH
		1♣¹	1♡
pass	3♡	pass	4♡
all pass			

1. Natural when a 1NT opening would show 12-14.

This auction occurred at rubber bridge and North's raise was invitational rather than preemptive. In club and competition play, North might be able to make a jump cuebid in opener's suit (3♣) to show values and four-card heart support.

West leads the seven of clubs (top of a doubleton, second highest from three/four small or lowest from something like K-8-7) and East plays the queen. How will you manage the play?

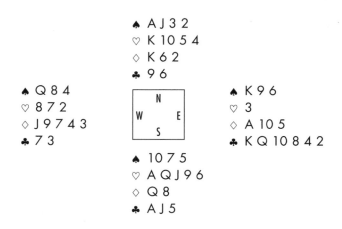

　　　　　　　♠ A J 3 2
　　　　　　　♡ K 10 5 4
　　　　　　　◇ K 6 2
　　　　　　　♣ 9 6

♠ Q 8 4　　　　　　　　　　　♠ K 9 6
♡ 8 7 2　　　　　　　　　　　♡ 3
◇ J 9 7 4 3　　　　　　　　　◇ A 10 5
♣ 7 3　　　　　　　　　　　　♣ K Q 10 8 4 2

　　　　　　　♠ 10 7 5
　　　　　　　♡ A Q J 9 6
　　　　　　　◇ Q 8
　　　　　　　♣ A J 5

East has opened 1♣ and you play in 4♡ on a club lead.

You have a certain loser in each of the minor suits, so you can ill afford to lose two spades. The bidding makes it unlikely that West holds the ♠K-Q, as then East would have at most 10 points for the opening bid. If West has one of these cards and the suit breaks 4-2, a correct guess as to which defender has the doubleton will allow you to set up a trick by attacking the suit. Of course, you would prefer to force the opposition to do so.

The 1♣ opening more or less marks East with the ♣K-Q and the ace of diamonds (and if West has the club king, you stand little chance, as then East surely holds the ♠K-Q). Can you arrange to throw East in at the right moment?

Since you want to choose when to play a third round of clubs, you start by ducking the first club and finessing the jack on the return. (If East switched to a trump instead of continuing clubs, you would use the first of dummy's trump entries to take the finesse for yourself.) You then draw trumps, ending in dummy, and lead a small diamond to the queen. East must duck, as otherwise you will discard a spade on the king of diamonds. When in hand with the queen of diamonds, cash the ace of clubs, discarding a diamond from dummy. Now a diamond exit leaves East stuck.

Recover from Shock

♠ 9 3
♡ Q 10 8 5 4 3 2
◇ A
♣ 8 6 5

♣ 10 led

W   N   E
        S

♠ K 7 5
♡ A 7 6
◇ J 10 9 3
♣ A K J

Dealer South
Both vul.

WEST	NORTH	EAST	SOUTH
			1NT[1]
2♠	4◇[2]	pass	4♡
all pass			

1. 15-17.
2. Transfer to hearts.

After a hypermodern transfer sequence has cleverly placed the declaration in the strong hand, West leads a club, which runs to the queen and ace.

You don't see any problems? That makes it just the time to consider what might go wrong.

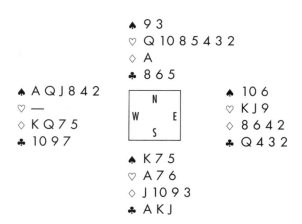

♠ 9 3
♥ Q 10 8 5 4 3 2
♦ A
♣ 8 6 5

♠ A Q J 8 4 2
♥ —
♦ K Q 7 5
♣ 10 9 7

♠ 10 6
♥ K J 9
♦ 8 6 4 2
♣ Q 4 3 2

♠ K 7 5
♥ A 7 6
♦ J 10 9 3
♣ A K J

You play in 4♡ after West has overcalled 2♠ and the initial club lead has solved one problem for you.

Now the contract is only in danger if you lose two trump tricks in addition to two spades. Given West's spade bid and failure to lead the suit, it seems highly probable that the ace of spades sits over your king. So, if the trumps lie badly, establishing a second winner in diamonds represents by far your best hope. With this in mind you should immediately lead a diamond to the ace. Then, when you return to the ace of hearts, you discover that East does indeed have two trump winners.

You next lead the nine of diamonds, intending to run it. If West covers this (by no means certain), ruff in dummy, return to hand with a club and lead another diamond. Again, if West covers, you ruff in dummy and now you must risk playing a third round of clubs. Eventually you discard a spade from dummy on a good diamond. After the initial shock in the trump suit, all has gone well and you and partner can congratulate yourselves on the bidding.

Of course, you would have been an entry short to set up a diamond if you had neglected to unblock the ace before testing trumps. This just goes to show the importance of considering the possibility of a bad break while you still have time to recover.

Boldly Bid

```
              ♠ Q 9
              ♡ Q 9 3
              ◇ A 8 7 6 5 2
              ♣ A 4
                    ┌──────────┐
                    │    N     │
  ♠A led            │ W      E │
                    │    S     │
                    └──────────┘
              ♠ 2
              ♡ A K J 10 6 4
              ◇ K J
              ♣ Q 9 6 2
```

Dealer North
Both vul.

WEST	NORTH	EAST	SOUTH
	1◇	pass	1♡
3♠	pass	pass	dbl
pass	4♡	pass	4NT
pass	5♠	pass	6♡
all pass			

With your heart holding, some would jump shift to 2♡ over partner's opening bid, which would be fair enough. Your subsequent
double was competitive. You took a slight chance on the club
position when you bid 4NT, but all was well when dummy
appeared. North's 5♠ indicated two keycards (here aces) and the
♡Q.

West led the ace of spades, and then a small spade to East's
king. Now, as South, you need to justify the bold bidding. How
should you set about the play?

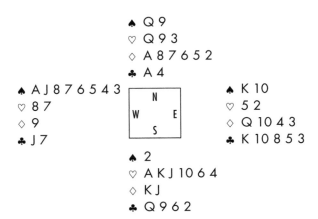

```
              ♠ Q 9
              ♡ Q 9 3
              ◇ A 8 7 6 5 2
              ♣ A 4
♠ A J 8 7 6 5 4 3          ♠ K 10
♡ 8 7            N          ♡ 5 2
◇ 9         W        E      ◇ Q 10 4 3
♣ J 7            S          ♣ K 10 8 5 3
              ♠ 2
              ♡ A K J 10 6 4
              ◇ K J
              ♣ Q 9 6 2
```

Had you reached 6♡ with no adverse bidding, the natural line would be as follows: ruff the second spade, draw two rounds of trumps and then play diamonds, hoping for a 3-2 split.

In practice, West's vulnerable preemptive overcall (and East's disinterest in competing further) may incline you to read the spades as 8-2. In this case, if West turns up with two or three trumps, it is surely right to play for an uneven diamond division. Furthermore, a small singleton diamond will occur far more often than a singleton queen.

After ruffing the second spade, play the ace of hearts and a heart to the nine. Everybody has followed to two rounds of trumps, so you boldly finesse the jack of diamonds, playing East for ◇Q-x-x-x. When West can only produce the nine you are home. Cash the king of diamonds, cross to the queen of hearts and ruff a small diamond. You have now set up dummy's suit and the ace of clubs will provide an entry to the winners there.

Yes, an early club switch would have defeated the contract. 'You might have held the singleton spade,' West remarked. Perhaps, but in that case you would hold ♠K-2 doubleton and would probably have dropped the king of spades under the ace.

Divide and Rule

```
              ♠ Q 4
              ♡ J 10 9 2
              ◇ J 9 6 3
              ♣ Q 7 5

                   N
              W         E
                   S

♠J led

              ♠ A K 6 3
              ♡ A K Q 5 3
              ◇ K 2
              ♣ 8 6
```

Dealer South
Both vul.

WEST	NORTH	EAST	SOUTH
			1♡
1♠	2♡	pass	4♡
all pass			

West leads the jack of spades and dummy's queen holds. All follow to two rounds of trumps.

Bearing in mind that West would hardly overcall on a bad suit and a bad hand, especially when vulnerable, how will you play now to avoid losing two diamonds and two clubs?

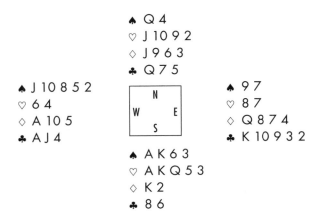

To make a vulnerable overcall on a jack-high suit West surely holds good values in the minors. However, most people would lead a club from A-K in preference to a spade from J-10, so you should put East with one of the top clubs. This means you might go down in four hearts, losing two tricks in each minor.

Luckily, the 2-2 trump break provides an extra chance. Take two more rounds of spades, discarding a *club* from dummy on the third round. Then ruff the fourth round and exit with a club. After winning two clubs, the defenders can do no better than play a diamond and you should have no problem taking the right view, placing West with the ace rather than the queen.

On this deal, you could not draw much inference from which defender won the second round of clubs. Now suppose in a similar situation you need to avoid any diamond losers:

```
             ◇ Q 10 6 3
  ◇ J 9 5                    ◇ K 8 7 4
             ◇ A 2
```

On the lead of the five, you should play dummy's ten since if West had the king East would have arranged to be on lead.

Light Cover

```
        ♠ 9 7 4
        ♡ J 2
        ◇ K J 9 7 5
        ♣ A 10 2
```

♠ 3 led

```
        N
    W       E
        S
```

```
        ♠ A J 6
        ♡ A Q 10 5
        ◇ 6 4 3 2
        ♣ K Q
```

Dealer East
N–S vul.

WEST	NORTH	EAST	SOUTH
		1♡	1NT
pass	3NT	all pass	

If the bottom of the range for your overcall is 15 points (and few players like to pass with that much), North's holding seems only just worth the raise to game. Of course, the five-card suit with a sure outside entry is a positive feature and knowing where most of the missing values lie often assists declarer in the play.

No doubt expecting you to be ready for a heart lead, West tables the three of spades. East plays the king. It looks like you have decisions to make in spades and diamonds. How will you manage them?

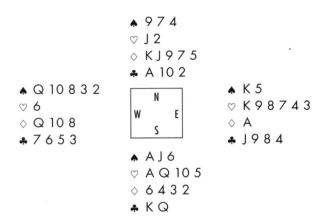

You are in 3NT on a spade lead after East has opened 1♡.

There is probably no shortage of winners, so you direct your attention to avoiding the loss of three or four spades and two diamonds. Since the opening bid places the ace of diamonds on your right, it will prove impossible to keep East out of the lead. You therefore duck the spade lead. Then, just in case the suit is breaking 4-3, you play the jack on the spade return and win the third round, as East shows out.

The problem now is to develop the diamonds without letting West gain the lead. To do this, simply lead a diamond and cover whatever West plays. You will not mind losing two tricks in the suit if East has A-10 and West Q-8.

This position is similar if more spectacular:

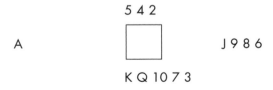

If you can afford to lose two tricks in this suit but not for East to gain the lead, you can take a first-round finesse of the seven! This saves the day if West holds the singleton ace.

Empty Air

```
        ♠ 8 5 4
        ♡ K J 3
        ◇ A 6 5
        ♣ A 7 5 4

              ┌─────────┐
              │    N    │
♠A led        │ W     E │
              │    S    │
              └─────────┘

        ♠ Q J
        ♡ A 10 9 8 7 6
        ◇ K 4
        ♣ K 6 3
```

Dealer South
E–W vul.

WEST	NORTH	EAST	SOUTH
			1♡
1♠	2♠	pass	4♡
all pass			

You are playing five-card majors and North's cuebid of 2♠ shows a value raise with three or more trumps and at least sufficient strength to invite game.

West begins with the ace and king of spades and continues with the ten, on which East discards a small diamond. How will you play? Much seems to depend on the position of the queen of hearts.

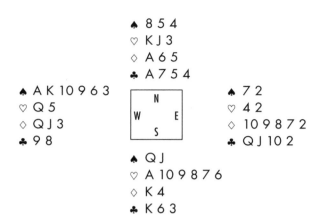

```
                    ♠ 8 5 4
                    ♡ K J 3
                    ◇ A 6 5
                    ♣ A 7 5 4
  ♠ A K 10 9 6 3       ┌─────────┐      ♠ 7 2
  ♡ Q 5                │    N    │      ♡ 4 2
  ◇ Q J 3              │ W     E │      ◇ 10 9 8 7 2
  ♣ 9 8                │    S    │      ♣ Q J 10 2
                       └─────────┘
                    ♠ Q J
                    ♡ A 10 9 8 7 6
                    ◇ K 4
                    ♣ K 6 3
```

You are playing in 4♡ and West leads three rounds of spades,
East showing out on the third round.

After ruffing the third spade, a player aware of the theory of
vacant spaces (that a defender short in one suit often has length
in another and vice versa) might lead a heart to the king and
finesse on the way back. An apology would be in order. 'Sorry,
partner, but I knew the spades were 6-2, so West was quite likely
to hold a singleton trump.'

You need to play with more subtlety. After playing the same
way to the first four tricks, turn to diamonds. Take the king, the
ace and ruff the third round. If you get overruffed, you are no
worse off than if you took the trump finesse. When all follow,
continue with the ♣K and a small club. After the ace wins you
can run the ♡J safely, because West, upon winning with the
queen, must concede a ruff and discard.

You need not worry about a ruff on the second diamond or
second club. In this case West will be ruffing empty air and you
will make the rest of the tricks.

In practical terms, the above line only backfires if East has six
diamonds and four clubs. In that case, if you left diamonds
alone, you could afford to lose a trump because East would suc-
cumb to a squeeze in the minors. Clearly, the actual layout is
more likely.

∩ecessary Assumption

```
              ♠ A Q 6
              ♡ J 10 9 4
              ◇ 7 6
              ♣ A Q 7 2

                    N
♣6 led        W           E
                    S

              ♠ J 10 9 8 3 2
              ♡ K 5
              ◇ J 9 3
              ♣ 4 3
```

Dealer West
Both vul.

WEST	NORTH	EAST	SOUTH
pass	1♣	pass	1♠
pass	2♠	pass	pass
3◇	pass	pass	3♠
all pass			

At this vulnerability, a 1NT opening would be 15-17, so partner opened 1♣. His decision to raise spades was definitely best with three good spades and a ruffing value. West stepped in with 3◇, aware that it rarely pays to sell out at the two-level when the points are evenly distributed and the other side has found a fit. Your decision to bid on to 3♠ is reasonable with the known nine-card (or better) fit.

West leads the six of clubs. You try dummy's queen but East wins with the king and switches to the two of hearts. Which heart do you play from hand, and why?

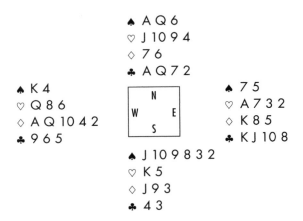

                        ♠ A Q 6
                        ♡ J 10 9 4
                        ◊ 7 6
                        ♣ A Q 7 2
    ♠ K 4   ♠ 7 5
    ♡ Q 8 6   N   ♡ A 7 3 2
    ◊ A Q 10 4 2   W   E   ◊ K 8 5
    ♣ 9 6 5   S   ♣ K J 10 8
                        ♠ J 10 9 8 3 2
                        ♡ K 5
                        ◊ J 9 3
                        ♣ 4 3

You play in 3♠ after West has made a delayed overcall in diamonds. A low club lead goes to the queen and king and East
switches to the two of hearts.

Now that the club finesse has gone wrong you have four top
losers, so you must start by presuming the spade finesse will
work. From that point, how will you reconstruct the defending
hands? Remember that West has passed as dealer.

Could letting the heart run to the jack be right? West might
hold something like this:

    ♠ K x   ♡ A x x   ◊ K 10 x x x   ♣ x x x

This hand seems consistent enough with the bidding. However,
you have to create a rather special distribution for the ace of
hearts to sit on your left. More likely West has a fair suit of diamonds, headed by the ace-queen (and hence no ♡A).

The original declarer misguessed the situation, arguing that
East might have hesitated to lead a small heart from the ace lest
declarer hold a singleton king. Maybe you can see the answer to
that. With 4-5 in the red suits, West would have doubled 2♠ for
takeout rather than overcalling 3◊.

Almost No Problem

```
         ♠ A 10 5 4
         ♡ K J 10
         ◇ K 4
         ♣ Q J 3 2

              N
◇ Q led   W       E
              S

         ♠ K J 9 6 2
         ♡ A 5 4
         ◇ 9
         ♣ 9 7 6 5
```

Dealer East
E–W vul.

WEST	NORTH	EAST	SOUTH
		3◇	pass
pass	dbl	pass	4♠
all pass			

You have only 8 points in high cards — about what North expected — but the five-card major, prime values and singleton diamond justify the jump to 4♠.

West leads the queen of diamonds. To encourage a diamond continuation you cover with dummy's king. East wins and returns the ten of diamonds, which you ruff.

Having got in, you play king and another spade. You are prepared to finesse, but you find West with Q-x. What do you do next?

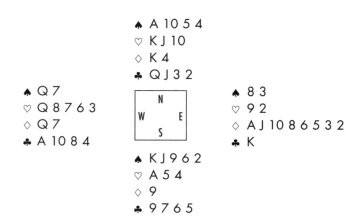

You are playing in 4♠ after East, who is vulnerable against not, opened 3◇ as dealer. You ruff the second round of diamonds and draw trumps in two rounds.

The first question is whether to play on clubs or try to guess the hearts. If you come to hand with a trump and lead a club to the queen, one of two things will happen. If West has A-10-8-4 or K-10-8-4 then East will win and exit with a heart and you will have two more club losers. Alternatively, if the clubs break 3-2, East will win your club lead and return the suit, leaving you to guess the heart position.

From this you can conclude that it cannot cost to tackle the hearts yourself, coming over to the ace and finessing West for the queen. After successfully negotiating three rounds of hearts, you enter hand with a trump and play a club to the queen. If this loses and a club comes back then the suit is breaking evenly and you have no worries. In practice, East, after winning with the king, has to lead a diamond, conceding a ruff and discard. In comparison to some of the other challenges in this book, you might say there is almost no problem on this deal.

No Triple Play

```
        ♠ K 4
        ♡ A 7 6
        ◇ K 7 5 4 2
        ♣ K 7 5
```

	N	
W		E
	S	

♡ Q led

```
        ♠ Q 9 8 7 3 2
        ♡ 9 3
        ◇ A 6 3
        ♣ A 6
```

Dealer East
N–S vul.

WEST	NORTH	EAST	SOUTH
		1NT[1]	2♠
pass	4♠	all pass	

1. 12-14.

You have made a questionable overcall at the vulnerability and cannot complain about your partner's raise to game.

West leads the queen of hearts — not good news, as the chance of finding A-x of trumps on your left has just shrunk from a slim chance to zero. West could possibly hold J-10 doubleton, of course, but otherwise it looks as though you have four certain losers. A little technical knowledge may come in useful here.

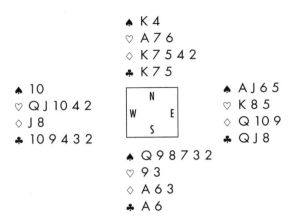

```
              ♠ K 4
              ♡ A 7 6
              ◇ K 7 5 4 2
              ♣ K 7 5
♠ 10                        ♠ A J 6 5
♡ Q J 10 4 2        N       ♡ K 8 5
◇ J 8          W         E   ◇ Q 10 9
♣ 10 9 4 3 2        S       ♣ Q J 8
              ♠ Q 9 8 7 3 2
              ♡ 9 3
              ◇ A 6 3
              ♣ A 6
```

You play in 4♠ after East has opened a 12-14 1NT and West leads the queen of hearts. Apart from the queen and jack of hearts, the defenders hold only 14 points between them, so East must have the ace of spades.

The chance of a squeeze for your tenth trick appears minimal and an attack on entries could destroy them altogether. The only real hope lies in avoiding two trump losers. Sometimes you can lose only one trick to an opposing 10-x and A-J-x, but that would involve a triple trump reduction and an end position you could not reach here. (For it to work you would need dummy to hold a fourth heart or a fourth club rather than a fifth diamond.)

Finding West with the jack or ten of spades alone represents your best bet (more likely than J-10 doubleton). Duck the first heart and win the likely heart continuation. Then ruff a heart and lead a spade to the ten and king. Subsequently you can use dummy's remaining entries to finesse the nine of spades and then ruff a club. After cashing any winners left in the side suits, you exit with a diamond. This is only your third trick lost and you will take the last two tricks with the Q-8 of spades over J-x.

Assuming the spades are as you want them, the trump coup also works if East has any 4432 type (or even 4-5-2-2, as long as you are careful enough to cash your second diamond winner before ruffing the third club).

Blithe Spirit

```
          ♠ K Q 6
          ♡ A 9 8 5
          ◇ K 8
          ♣ A 9 8 3
```

```
                    ┌─────────┐
                    │    N    │
  ◇ Q led           │ W     E │
                    │    S    │
                    └─────────┘
```

```
          ♠ J 10 8 7 4 2
          ♡ J 3
          ◇ 10 6 4
          ♣ J 2
```

Dealer West
Neither vul.

WEST	NORTH	EAST	SOUTH
1NT[1]	dbl[2]	pass	2♠
all pass			

1. 12-14.
2. Penalties, implying at least 15 points.

Not being on lead and having no likely entry, you correctly remove the double. When dummy appears you see that 1NT doubled might go off; it would depend on whether West has three spades or two and how early your side led the suit.

West's lead of the ◇Q in front of the strong hand might be from something like A-Q-9-x, but you consider that unlikely here. Assuming East has the ◇A and the defenders lead trumps each time they get the chance, you could have six losers — three in diamonds and one in every other suit. What is your plan?

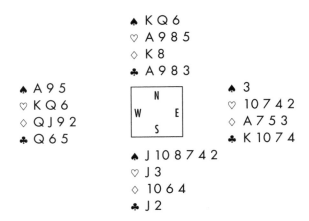

♠ K Q 6
♡ A 9 8 5
◇ K 8
♣ A 9 8 3

♠ A 9 5
♡ K Q 6
◇ Q J 9 2
♣ Q 6 5

♠ 3
♡ 10 7 4 2
◇ A 7 5 3
♣ K 10 7 4

♠ J 10 8 7 4 2
♡ J 3
◇ 10 6 4
♣ J 2

West, who opened a weak notrump, led the queen of diamonds against 2♠. The original declarer blithely covered. East won with the ace and the defenders played two rounds of trumps. After getting back in with the next round of diamonds, West led a third round of trumps. This left declarer with three more losers, so the contract went one down and North was not pleased.

An argument followed as to whether ducking the first diamond would help. Say that West finds the best continuation: ace and another spade. After that, the king of diamonds loses to the ace and East tries a small heart, which runs to the queen and ace. The next heart loses to the king and West leads a third trump, preventing the diamond ruff. You overcome this by running the ♡9-8 through East's ♡10-7 on a ruffing finesse to set up an eighth trick. A similar position (and end result) develops if East, upon getting in with the ace of diamonds, leads a club.

As the play actually went (with the first diamond lost to East), the original declarer could have succeeded by playing a small heart from hand after winning the second round of trumps with the jack. Needless to say, this was not an obvious play to make.

♠ K 8 6 5
♡ 8 4
◊ K J 10 3 2
♣ K 9

♠ Q led

```
    N
W       E
    S
```

♠ —
♡ K Q J 10 9 7 5
◊ Q 5 4
♣ Q 10 2

Dealer West
E–W vul.

WEST	NORTH	EAST	SOUTH
1♠	pass	3♠¹	4♡
all pass			

1. Four-card limit raise.

When one side is bidding spades and the other is bidding hearts, the former usually manages to buy the contract. As they say, the exception proves the rule; in this case the vulnerability and matchpoint scoring no doubt played a part.

West leads the queen of spades. You play low from dummy and ruff with the nine on general principles. How should you continue?

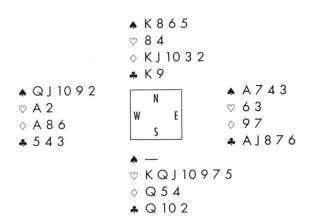

♠ K 8 6 5
♡ 8 4
◇ K J 10 3 2
♣ K 9

♠ Q J 10 9 2
♡ A 2
◇ A 8 6
♣ 5 4 3

N
W E
S

♠ A 7 4 3
♡ 6 3
◇ 9 7
♣ A J 8 7 6

♠ —
♡ K Q J 10 9 7 5
◇ Q 5 4
♣ Q 10 2

Although the opponents have played to only one trick and made only two bids — 1♠ and 3♠ — you know quite a lot about their hands. West must have five spades to the queen-jack and East four to the ace. You can also place them with two aces each — West would be too weak to open with only one and would have bid 4♠ with three.

You have three top losers in four hearts and two easy ways to avoid a slow club loser. For one, if the ace of diamonds is doubleton, whoever has it will be unable to hold up twice. For another, dummy's king of clubs might provide an important entry. If both chances fail, the fly in the ointment will be the jack of clubs, which either defender could hold.

A clever line of play, very difficult to foresee, overcomes this hazard. After ruffing the opening lead with the nine of hearts, lead low to dummy's eight. If the eight is captured by East's ace, dummy's club king will certainly provide the late entry to diamonds. Then you ruff a spade and lead a second trump. West wins with the ace and does best to exit with a small diamond. You take this in dummy with the ten and ruff a third round of spades. Next, overtake the queen of diamonds with the king and exit with the king of spades, discarding your remaining diamond. Now East has to open up the clubs.

Trick from Nowhere

```
        ♠ 10 9 5 4 3
        ♡ Q 10 7
        ◇ A 9 8
        ♣ 9 2

              N
♣ K led    W     E
              S

        ♠ A Q 8 6 2
        ♡ K 6 4 3
        ◇ Q J 2
        ♣ A
```

Dealer South
Both vul.

WEST	NORTH	EAST	SOUTH
			1♠
1NT	2♠	pass	3♡
pass	4♠	all pass	

With a five-loser hand, you can hardly do less than try for game, even though West's 1NT overcall suggests that any finesse in trumps will lose and the suit might break badly. Those factors aside, knowledge of how the cards are likely to lie often helps in the play. North, with five-card support and two useful cards in the red suits, obviously accepts the invitation.

West leads the king of clubs against four spades and the first sight of the dummy gives only modest cause for optimism. West may well hold two trump tricks.

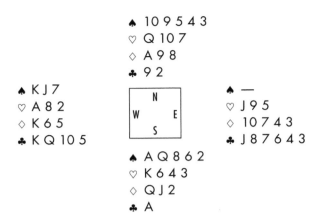

♠ 10 9 5 4 3
♡ Q 10 7
◇ A 9 8
♣ 9 2

♠ K J 7
♡ A 8 2
◇ K 6 5
♣ K Q 10 5

N
W E
S

♠ —
♡ J 9 5
◇ 10 7 4 3
♣ J 8 7 6 4 3

♠ A Q 8 6 2
♡ K 6 4 3
◇ Q J 2
♣ A

Prospects do not seem good when West leads the king of clubs against 4♠. Trumps may well break 3-0, giving two losers there, and you face the danger of losing two hearts and a diamond as well. A glance at the diagram will justify most of your fears. Even so, West will find it difficult to defend with so little help from East.

After winning the first club trick, advance the queen of diamonds. West, placing you with the jack (unless you have a reputation as a devious character), does best to duck. You continue with a heart to the queen — no need to finesse at this point — ruff a club and exit with the queen of spades.

Upon winning with the king, West will find that nothing in the garden looks lovely. A club lead will allow you to ruff in hand and discard a heart from dummy. You can then lead the king of hearts, setting up a long heart for a diamond discard when the suit breaks 3-3. (You would also be fine if the heart ace were now singleton, as West would be hopelessly endplayed.)

If, having exited the first time in trumps, you get a lead into a tenace — hearts, diamonds or even spades — you can still cope. This will give you one trick at once and you can always put West back on lead and gain another trick from nowhere.

Count Will Tell

```
         ♠ A Q 8
         ♡ K J 10 8 7
         ◇ 10 6 2
         ♣ J 8

                  ┌─────────┐
                  │    N    │
  ♣ 6 led         │ W     E │
                  │    S    │
                  └─────────┘

         ♠ K 10 2
         ♡ A Q 6
         ◇ A J 7 5
         ♣ 9 5 4
```

Dealer East
Neither vul.

WEST	NORTH	EAST	SOUTH
		pass	1NT
pass	2◇	pass	2♡
pass	3NT	pass	4♡
all pass			

The 14-16 range for a 1NT opening is popular with some top players, notably England's Tony Forrester. With good support for the suit into which North transferred and not having a club stopper, you prefer the heart game to 3NT.

West leads the six of clubs to East's king. East cashes the ace of clubs, on which West plays the two, and leads a third club, which you ruff in dummy. From West's echo (implying a holding of Q-10-x-x-x) it looks like you have done well to avoid 3NT, but can you make 4♡?

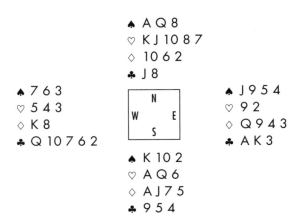

```
              ♠ A Q 8
              ♡ K J 10 8 7
              ◇ 10 6 2
              ♣ J 8
♠ 7 6 3          ┌─────────┐          ♠ J 9 5 4
♡ 5 4 3          │    N    │          ♡ 9 2
◇ K 8            │ W     E │          ◇ Q 9 4 3
♣ Q 10 7 6 2     │    S    │          ♣ A K 3
                 └─────────┘
              ♠ K 10 2
              ♡ A Q 6
              ◇ A J 7 5
              ♣ 9 5 4
```

You opened a 14-16 notrump in second seat and play in 4♡. The defenders lead three rounds of clubs.

The problem is to avoid losing two diamonds. Since not many people would pass as dealer with 12 points, especially when non-vulnerable, you can infer that East, who has played the A-K of clubs, cannot hold the ◇K-Q.

On certain layouts, you might achieve an elimination type of endplay. In essence, you would need to find West with the ◇K-Q, a doubleton in trumps and either three or four spades. This seems a bit of a tall order.

Instead, you should try to get a count of the distribution, which will tell you how to tackle the diamonds. Take two rounds of trumps with the ace and jack. When all follow, draw the last trump and cash three rounds of spades.

You already know about the 5-3 club division, and if West produces five or more cards in the majors, only East can hold four diamonds. In this case, play West for the doubleton king or queen, perhaps leading the ten from dummy. If East covers with the queen, you can duck and rise with the ace next time.

Had West turned out to be short in the majors you would have led a small diamond from dummy, playing East for Q-x or K-x.

```
         ♠ A Q 5
         ♡ 10
         ◇ K Q 10 8 5 2
         ♣ K 7 5

              ┌─────────┐
              │    N    │
  ♡ K led     │  W   E  │
              │    S    │
              └─────────┘

         ♠ K 8 3
         ♡ J 8 5 3 2
         ◇ A 3
         ♣ A 10 2
```

Dealer West
N–S vul.

WEST	NORTH	EAST	SOUTH
2◇	3◇	pass	3NT
all pass			

Playing Precision or two-over-one, a minimum opening with a 4-5-2-2 shape presents a problem. What can you rebid if you open one heart and partner makes a forcing 1NT response?

One solution (though not the best in Mike Lawrence's view or mine) is Flannery, by which a two diamond opening shows any opening hand with 4-5 in the majors and too weak to reverse.

West leads the king of hearts (a strong lead in their methods, requesting a count signal or unblock) and East plays the seven. West switches to the jack of spades. No problem will arise if the diamonds break 3-2, but suppose East has J-x-x-x — quite likely if West has nine cards in the majors. What will you do then?

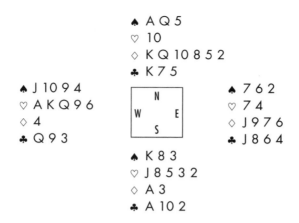

♠ A Q 5
♡ 10
◇ K Q 10 8 5 2
♣ K 7 5

♠ J 10 9 4
♡ A K Q 9 6
◇ 4
♣ Q 9 3

♠ 7 6 2
♡ 7 4
◇ J 9 7 6
♣ J 8 6 4

♠ K 8 3
♡ J 8 5 3 2
◇ A 3
♣ A 10 2

West, who has opened a 'Flannery' 2◇, showing four spades and five hearts, leads the ♡K against your 3NT contract. When East follows with the seven, West switches to the jack of spades. Naturally, you win with the ace before cashing two rounds of diamonds with the ace and king. Unfortunately, West discards a small heart on the second round, revealing that East started with four to the jack.

You cannot give up a diamond now, as another heart from East would presumably give West three more tricks in the suit. Strange though it may seem, the best play is to come to hand with the king of spades and walk into the lion's den by leading the eight of hearts!

West could cash three heart tricks at this point, but doing so would establish your jack for the ninth trick. West's best move is to cash two hearts only and then exit with a club. You can win this in dummy before letting East win a diamond. You make game with three spades, four diamonds and two clubs.

As the cards lie, you could also succeed if you won the first spade with the king, but then you would need to win the second round of diamonds in hand (or give up on the hope of overtricks by conceding a heart even before testing the diamonds).

No Guess Needed

♠ 10 4 3
♡ A K Q 6
◇ K 10 9 5
♣ 6 4

♣K led

♠ K Q
♡ 9 7 5 4 2
◇ Q 4
♣ A J 7 5

Dealer West
Neither vul.

WEST	NORTH	EAST	SOUTH
1NT[1]	pass	2♠	pass
pass	dbl	pass	4♡
all pass			

1. 10-12.

East-West are playing what is known as the 'mini' 1NT at this vulnerability. Some might judge another adjective more suitable: kamikaze. Whatever its merits, it nearly succeeded in keeping your side out of the bidding.

West leads the king of clubs, which you allow to hold. A low spade switch goes to the ace and East returns the nine of clubs to your ace. Assuming trumps do not split 4-0, you can count nine tricks — five trumps, a spade, a diamond, a club and a ruff. Can you be sure of developing a tenth?

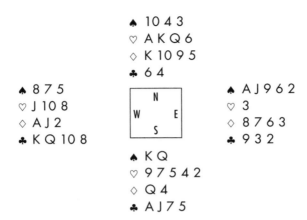

```
                    ♠ 10 4 3
                    ♡ A K Q 6
                    ◇ K 10 9 5
                    ♣ 6 4
    ♠ 8 7 5          ┌─────────┐      ♠ A J 9 6 2
    ♡ J 10 8         │    N    │      ♡ 3
    ◇ A J 2          │ W     E │      ◇ 8 7 6 3
    ♣ K Q 10 8       │    S    │      ♣ 9 3 2
                     └─────────┘
                    ♠ K Q
                    ♡ 9 7 5 4 2
                    ◇ Q 4
                    ♣ A J 7 5
```

West, who has opened a 'mini' 1NT, leads the king of clubs against 4♡. You allow this to hold and a small spade comes next. East, who has made a weak takeout into spades, wins with the ace and returns the nine of clubs to your ace.

You start by drawing trumps and note that West started with J-10-x and that East discarded two spades. The 3-1 break has prevented you from ruffing two diamonds in dummy and you are now a trick short. It looks as though the contract will depend upon finding the jack of diamonds. You cannot tell for sure who holds this vital card because West, remember, has announced 10-12 points and could have 10 points without it — the ♡J, the ◇A and ♣K-Q — or 11 or 12 points with it.

Luckily, you do not need to guess. Play a spade to hand and advance a small diamond. West must duck, because otherwise you will make the king and queen separately. In dummy with the king of diamonds, you ruff the third spade and then exit with the queen of diamonds. This forces West, upon winning this trick, to lead either a diamond or a club, either of which provides your tenth trick.

Offer No Chance

♠ Q 8 7 3
♡ 9 3 2
◇ 10 9 7
♣ A K 10

♡ 6 led

```
        N
    W       E
        S
```

♠ K 9
♡ A J 7
◇ K Q 8 6 5
♣ Q 7 5

Dealer East
E–W vul.

WEST	NORTH	EAST	SOUTH
		1 ♠	1NT
pass	3NT	all pass	

You had a slightly awkward choice of overcall. The hand is too flat, really, for a two-level overcall and a takeout double will all too often lead to playing in a 4-3 fit. Despite the inflexibility of the spade stopper, 1NT describes the nature and strength of the hand well and is probably best.

You need not have worried about the questionable spade holding, as West leads the six of hearts and East plays the king. You hold off and East returns the five of hearts. Should you win this trick or not — and why?

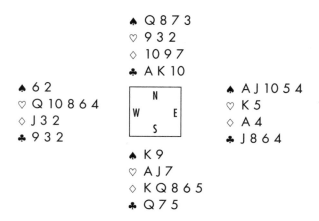

```
              ♠ Q 8 7 3
              ♡ 9 3 2
              ◊ 10 9 7
              ♣ A K 10
♠ 6 2                        ♠ A J 10 5 4
♡ Q 10 8 6 4    N            ♡ K 5
◊ J 3 2      W     E         ◊ A 4
♣ 9 3 2          S           ♣ J 8 6 4
              ♠ K 9
              ♡ A J 7
              ◊ K Q 8 6 5
              ♣ Q 7 5
```

After East has opened 1♠, you arrive in 3NT. West leads a small heart and you allow the king to win. East returns the five of hearts and you must decide what to do.

The opening bid of 1♠ marks East with both the missing aces. This knowledge should enable you to play the diamonds to best advantage and shut out West's hearts.

You might think of ducking the second heart on the grounds that if hearts are 4-3 you will be in danger of losing three hearts and two aces. However, it seems very unlikely that West, with a weak hand, would lead from four hearts to the queen-ten in preference to East's suit.

Can you see why ducking the second round of hearts might place the contract in jeopardy? West might lead a third round of hearts and East, aiming to create an entry to the long hearts, might discard the ace of diamonds!

So win the second round of hearts, cross to the king of clubs and lead a diamond to the queen. Then go back to the ace of clubs and play another diamond. East may win and play a third club, but the defenders will still make only two aces, one heart and the long club.

Not Forgiven

```
     ♠ A Q 7 4
     ♡ 9 6 5 3
     ◇ A J
     ♣ Q J 6
```

♡ 4 led

```
        N
     W     E
        S
```

```
     ♠ 6
     ♡ A Q
     ◇ K Q 9
     ♣ K 10 9 5 4 3 2
```

Dealer East
Both vul.

WEST	NORTH	EAST	SOUTH
		1♡	3♣
pass	3♡	pass	3NT
pass	4♣	pass	4♡
pass	4♠	pass	6♣
all pass			

At rubber bridge, you are happy to be playing strong jump over-calls. In the traditional style of cuebidding, both 4♡ and 4♠ indicated first-round controls.

West leads the four of hearts, which goes to the eight and queen. As South, how should you plan the play?

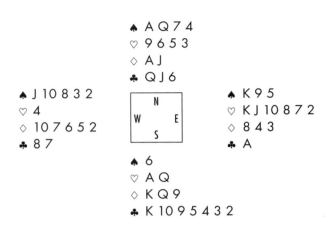

<table>
<tr><td></td><td>♠ A Q 7 4</td><td></td></tr>
<tr><td></td><td>♡ 9 6 5 3</td><td></td></tr>
<tr><td></td><td>◇ A J</td><td></td></tr>
<tr><td></td><td>♣ Q J 6</td><td></td></tr>
</table>

♠ J 10 8 3 2   ♠ K 9 5
♡ 4   ♡ K J 10 8 7 2
◇ 10 7 6 5 2   ◇ 8 4 3
♣ 8 7   ♣ A

♠ 6
♡ A Q
◇ K Q 9
♣ K 10 9 5 4 3 2

You have reached 6♣ after an opening bid of 1♡ by East. You win the first trick with the queen of hearts.

West might have started with 4-2 doubleton in hearts or a singleton trump, but otherwise you had better take care. If you start on the trump suit and run into a heart ruff, then even if you could forgive yourself, partner might not (especially playing for money).

It surely costs nothing to cross to the ace of spades and ruff a spade. Continue with a diamond to the jack and ruff another spade. When the king falls, you return to dummy with the ace of diamonds and lead the queen of spades. East can only ruff with the ace of clubs and you discard your ace of hearts. If East can ruff low, that will not create a problem, as in this case you can overruff and return a trump in complete safety, knowing that West cannot have a second trump with which to ruff a heart.

An interesting sidelight is that if East held a 4-6-1-2 shape, it would be a brilliant move to play the king of spades on the third round of the suit, inducing declarer to run into a diamond ruff. Thankfully, few people defend that mischievously.

Slow Burn

```
            ♠ J 10 6
            ♡ K 7 3
            ◇ A 10 9 3
            ♣ J 7 4

                  ┌─────────┐
                  │    N    │
♣6 led            │ W     E │
                  │    S    │
                  └─────────┘

            ♠ A Q 9 8 3 2
            ♡ A 6
            ◇ J 8 7 2
            ♣ K
```

Dealer North
E–W vul.

WEST	NORTH	EAST	SOUTH
	pass	pass	1♠
pass	2♠	pass	3◇
pass	4♠	all pass	

Knowing that 6421 types generally provide a good source of tricks, you make a long-suit game try after the single raise. North, with a maximum in terms of high cards and some help in diamonds, happily accepts the invitation to go on.

West leads the six of clubs, which you assume is fourth best. East wins with the ace and switches to the jack of hearts. Surely you will not go down in this contract, will you?

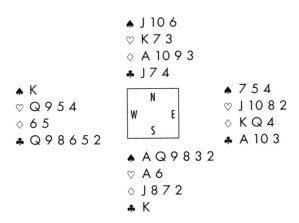

♠ J 10 6
♥ K 7 3
♦ A 10 9 3
♣ J 7 4

♠ K
♥ Q 9 5 4
♦ 6 5
♣ Q 9 8 6 5 2

♠ 7 5 4
♥ J 10 8 2
♦ K Q 4
♣ A 10 3

♠ A Q 9 8 3 2
♥ A 6
♦ J 8 7 2
♣ K

You open 1♠ in third position and finish in 4♠. West leads a club to the ace and East returns the jack of hearts.

At rubber bridge the original declarer, a charming gentleman known as Laurie, managed to go down, losing a club, a spade and two diamonds. It took the other players quite a long time to convince Laurie that he had not handled the play brilliantly. In essence, the point they made was as follows:

East, who passed in second position, cannot hold the king of spades, the ♡J-10, the ◊K-Q and the ace of clubs. It cannot cost, therefore, to lay down the ace of spades, dropping the king as the cards lie. If instead the trump finesse had been right, West would hold the king or queen of diamonds (or both, as a diamond lead was unattractive on the auction) and you would lose only one diamond trick.

Note that an initial heart lead might beat the contract. Yes, you could choose to play on clubs to find out who has the ace, but the risk of running into a diamond ruff (say if West has K-x of trumps and K-x or Q-x of diamonds and the defenders switch to diamonds) probably outweighs the potential benefit.

Guard the Exit

```
              ♠ 9 8 7
              ♡ K 9 2
              ◇ A 10 9 4
              ♣ K 8 3
           ┌─────────┐
           │    N    │
♠ 6 led    │ W     E │
           │    S    │
           └─────────┘
              ♠ A Q 5
              ♡ Q 8 3
              ◇ Q J 3 2
              ♣ A Q 7
```

Dealer East
Both vul.

WEST	NORTH	EAST	SOUTH
		1♠	1NT
pass	3NT	all pass	

Many good books on bidding highlight the weaknesses of a 4333
type. Here you can see why. You and partner possess 27 high
card points between you, yet, even with the spade finesse rating
to work, making nine tricks presents a challenge.

West leads the six of spades (top of a doubleton, most likely)
and East puts up the king. Will you win at once or will you hold
up? When you get in, how will you continue?

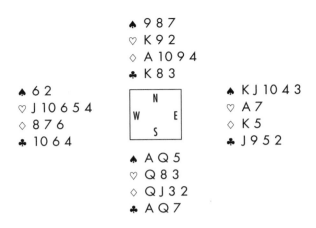

♠ 9 8 7
♡ K 9 2
◇ A 10 9 4
♣ K 8 3

♠ 6 2
♡ J 10 6 5 4
◇ 8 7 6
♣ 10 6 4

♠ K J 10 4 3
♡ A 7
◇ K 5
♣ J 9 5 2

♠ A Q 5
♡ Q 8 3
◇ Q J 3 2
♣ A Q 7

You play in 3NT after East has opened 1♠. West leads the six of spades and East plays the king.

If East-West are playing any standard system, you can read the six of spades as coming from a doubleton or singleton. In addition to five or six spades, East surely has the ace of hearts and the king of diamonds to justify opening the bidding. This means you do not expect to lose the lead to West. Indeed, holding up would be an error since it may prove vital to keep an exit card.

After winning the first spade trick, the natural play is to cross to the king of clubs and lead a low heart off dummy. If East woodenly ducks, you can win and set up the diamonds. A good player in the East seat will surely take the ace of hearts and persist with the spades. By this time you will have eight tricks on top and should plan to cash your winners in hearts and clubs before exiting in spades, forcing East to lead from ◇ K-x at the finish.

With a 5-3-2-3 shape, East could not counter this line of play. On the actual layout, it would be a good move to bare the ◇K nonchalantly when you cash the third round of hearts. You might go wrong in this case, but not if West is one of those players who consider it a duty always to signal length, playing low from an odd number and high-low with an even number.

Seeking Cover

```
        ♠ 8
        ♡ K J 8 6 5 2
        ◇ A 7 4 3
        ♣ Q 10
```

♣9 led

```
        N
      W   E
        S
```

```
        ♠ A K Q J 9 3
        ♡ —
        ◇ K Q 8
        ♣ 8 7 5 4
```

Dealer East
Both vul.

WEST	NORTH	EAST	SOUTH
		1♣	2♠¹
pass	3♡	pass	4♠
all pass			

1. Strong.

When West leads the nine of clubs you work out that you would
have had a club stopper in 3NT, but you cannot do much about
that now.

East wins with the jack, cashes the king and leads a small
club. As you rather feared, West ruffs with the ten of spades and
exits with a trump. How do you play from here?

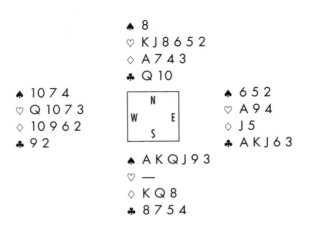

You play in 4♠ after East has opened 1♣. You lose two top clubs to East and then a club ruff to West, who now exits with a spade. West has defended well in working out that if you had a singleton heart you would not be able to win a fourth round of diamonds in dummy and discard it.

Any hope of a club ruff has vanished, but a 3-3 diamond break will still see you home. Also, with the position right for a squeeze, there will be no problem if East, who must guard the fourth round of clubs, has four diamonds. Assuming East would not go wrong if you won the trump switch in dummy and led a small heart, you can also gain a chance if West has length in diamonds.

Without the ace of hearts, East would not have much of an opening bid (especially when vulnerable), but you can hope that West has the queen. So let dummy's eight of spades win the switch and advance the king of hearts from dummy, forcing East to cover. This way dummy's jack of hearts will act as a menace against West's queen and any defender holding four diamonds will be unable to guard everything when you run the trumps. Now, unless West discards the queen of hearts, you will throw the jack of hearts from dummy on the final trump to keep four diamonds there for as long as possible.

Rare but Useful

```
            ♠ A 9 6 2
            ♡ Q 9 4 3
            ◇ K 7
            ♣ A Q 2
                 ┌─────────┐
                 │    N    │
◇ Q led          │ W     E │
                 │    S    │
                 └─────────┘

            ♠ Q 5 3
            ♡ A K J 10 6 2
            ◇ 10 3
            ♣ 6 5
```

Dealer South
Neither vul.

WEST	NORTH	EAST	SOUTH
			1♡
dbl	redbl	pass	2♡
pass	4♡	all pass	

Many Norths would prefer 2NT to a redouble, which would show four-card heart support and at least the values to invite game. However, if you are playing 2NT specifically as a limit raise (historically a popular treatment at rubber bridge and still common in North America), redouble is correct.

West leads the queen of diamonds — a disappointment for you. With the ace of diamonds offside, the club finesse should work, but how can you restrict your spade losers to one?

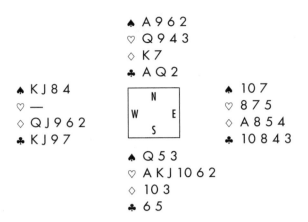

♠ A 9 6 2
♡ Q 9 4 3
◇ K 7
♣ A Q 2

♠ K J 8 4
♡ —
◇ Q J 9 6 2
♣ K J 9 7

♠ 10 7
♡ 8 7 5
◇ A 8 5 4
♣ 10 8 4 3

♠ Q 5 3
♡ A K J 10 6 2
◇ 10 3
♣ 6 5

When West, who doubled your opening bid of 1♡, leads the queen of diamonds against 4♡, you see four likely losers — two diamonds and two spades. At least the club finesse should succeed.

Just in case, you might as well cover the first diamond. After the defenders take two tricks in the suit, West leads the jack of clubs. As expected, dummy's queen wins.

All now depends on losing no more than one trick in spades. The original declarer took the ace of clubs, ruffed a club, drew three rounds of trumps ending in dummy and tried a small spade. When East played the seven there was no way to avoid losing two spade tricks.

This combination would catch out quite a few players. The best play is to draw trumps in three rounds, West discarding two diamonds and a club; then you can eliminate the clubs and advance the queen of spades. West has to cover and now East is left on play with the ten on the second round, obliged to concede a ruff and discard. Admittedly, if West held ♠K-J-10-x you could succeed by eliminating the suit and leading a small spade towards the nine. However, East will hold 10-x or J-x twice as often as a small doubleton.

Defensive Error

♠ J 9 3 2
♡ K 10 5 4
◇ 8 5
♣ A Q 5

◇ J led

```
      N
 W         E
      S
```

♠ K 4
♡ A Q J 8 7 2
◇ K 6 4
♣ 9 3

Dealer East
N–S vul.

WEST	NORTH	EAST	SOUTH
		pass	1♡
pass	3♡	pass	4♡
all pass			

May I mention a treatment used by several top Swedish pairs and espoused by my regular partner, Graham Allan? It is an intermediate-range two of a major opening. It covers hands with a fair six-card suit and a bit better than a minimum opening but that are not good enough for opening one of the suit and jumping to three over a simple response. Your hand qualifies.

You reach 4♡ and West leads the jack of diamonds. East wins with the ace and returns the suit, your king winning. How do you play from here? (Trumps break 2-1.)

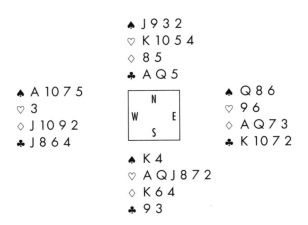

After opening 1♡ in second seat (or 2♡ if you are an instant convert to intermediate twos!) you play in 4♡. The jack of diamonds goes to East's ace and you win the second round with the king. You can draw trumps in two rounds and must consider how best to manage the black suits.

No problem will arise if the club finesse succeeds, so the declarer must consider what the situation will be if the king sits on the wrong side. In this case, East, who passed as dealer and who has already turned up with 6 points in diamonds, will not hold the ace of spades as well as the king of clubs.

You do not mind losing a spade trick to East, so the best play in the suit is to lead the four intending to play dummy's nine — not the jack, because West, if holding the queen, would win and switch to a club. As the cards lie, the nine forces the queen, allowing you to set up the jack of spades for a club discard.

Note that, as so often applies in such positions, East would have done better to duck the first round of diamonds, thereby establishing a quick entry to the West hand. It would have been very unlucky to find you with a singleton king.

A Question of Principle

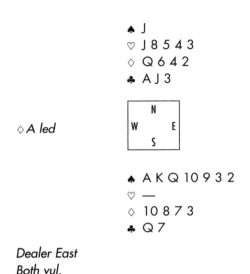

♠ J
♡ J 8 5 4 3
◇ Q 6 4 2
♣ A J 3

◇ A led

```
    N
W       E
    S
```

♠ A K Q 10 9 3 2
♡ —
◇ 10 8 7 3
♣ Q 7

Dealer East
Both vul.

WEST	NORTH	EAST	SOUTH
		1♡	4♠

all pass

West leads the ace of diamonds (ace from ace-king), East following with the nine. West continues with the diamond king, on which East discards a heart and then plays the jack, which is covered by the queen and ruffed. East tries to cash the ace of hearts, which would be the setting trick if you were not void, but you ruff. How are you coping with these developments?

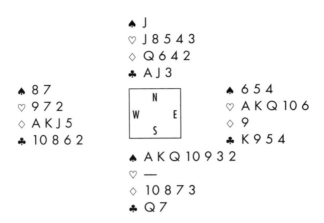

```
              ♠ J
              ♡ J 8 5 4 3
              ◇ Q 6 4 2
              ♣ A J 3
♠ 8 7                          ♠ 6 5 4
♡ 9 7 2          N             ♡ A K Q 10 6
◇ A K J 5    W       E         ◇ 9
♣ 10 8 6 2       S             ♣ K 9 5 4
              ♠ A K Q 10 9 3 2
              ♡ —
              ◇ 10 8 7 3
              ♣ Q 7
```

You play in 4♠ after East opened 1♡. West leads the ace and king of diamonds and plays a third round. East, who began with a singleton diamond, ruffs the third round and tries to cash the ace of hearts.

In view of East's opening bid (and West's failure to double 4♠), you can guarantee that the club finesse is wrong. This makes a squeeze the only real chance, a trump squeeze to be specific. As entries to the closed hand present no problem (you can simply ruff hearts), I trust that on the ◇A-K-J you unblocked the ◇10-8-7 on general principles.

After ruffing the heart, cross to the spade jack and ruff a heart high. Next, run all but one of your trumps, keeping two hearts, one diamond and the ♣A in dummy. Then cross to dummy by leading the splendidly preserved three of diamonds to the six. It should not be too difficult to judge whether East has come down to one heart and two clubs (when you ruff a heart), or two hearts and one club (when you cash the club ace). The singleton club is more likely, since East might hope that West holds the ♣Q.

Yes, if the defenders take their diamond ruff on the second round of the suit, you go down, but how could West know that the ◇9 was not top of a doubleton?

Two Ways to Win

♠ K J 10 6
♡ —
◊ Q 9 5 4
♣ K 10 7 5 3

♡A led

```
      N
  W       E
      S
```

♠ 5 3
♡ J 7 4
◊ A 10 6
♣ A Q J 8 2

Dealer East
Neither vul.

WEST	NORTH	EAST	SOUTH
		1♡	2♣
3♡	5♣	pass	pass
double	all pass		

At rubber bridge West's 3♡ is a limit raise, the same as it would be without the overcall. Many tournament players play a jump raise after intervention as preemptive and use a cuebid to show a raise based on values.

West leads the ace of hearts. Dummy ruffs and East plays the nine. Somehow, you must avoid losing two spades as well as a diamond. How will you do it?

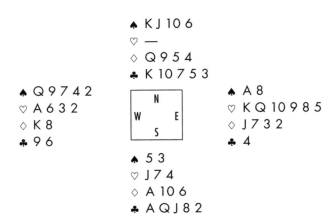

♠ K J 10 6
♡ —
◇ Q 9 5 4
♣ K 10 7 5 3

♠ Q 9 7 4 2
♡ A 6 3 2
◇ K 8
♣ 9 6

♠ A 8
♡ K Q 10 9 8 5
◇ J 7 3 2
♣ 4

♠ 5 3
♡ J 7 4
◇ A 10 6
♣ A Q J 8 2

East has opened 1♡ and West, who gave a limit jump raise, has doubled your contract of 5♣ and led the ♡A.

You start by ruffing the heart lead in dummy and coming to your hand with a trump, to which all follow. Dummy's trumps are fairly precious, so you should not lead a second round at this point.

You might think of tackling diamonds before spades, with the idea of playing for the ◇K and ♠A to lie in opposite hands. The trouble with that is you might lose two diamond tricks, in which case guessing the spades will not help. You do better to lead a spade and consider how to play when West follows low.

After West has produced the ace of hearts, it seems natural to play the opening bidder for the ace of spades and finesse the jack. As the cards lie, this lands the contract without further ado.

Now suppose that East holds the queen of spades and the king of diamonds, and West holds the ace of spades. Then the jack of spades loses to the queen. You ruff East's heart exit, return to hand with a trump and lead a second spade. What can West do now? Grabbing the ace establishes two discards, whilst ducking loses the ace, allowing you to play the diamonds for one loser, by leading the queen from dummy.

Let West Explain

```
            ♠ A K Q 3 2
            ♡ K Q
            ◇ 8 6 5
            ♣ 10 7 3
```

```
                    ┌─────────┐
                    │    N    │
♣6 led              │ W     E │
                    │    S    │
                    └─────────┘
```

```
            ♠ 8 7
            ♡ A 6 4
            ◇ Q J 10 4 3 2
            ♣ A 8
```

Dealer South
N–S vul.

WEST	NORTH	EAST	SOUTH
			1◇
pass	1♠	2NT	pass
3♡	4♡	pass	5◇
dbl	all pass		

East's 2NT was the ubiquitous Unusual Notrump, denoting length in the unbid suits. Particularly at this vulnerability, it may not show much in the way of values. North's cuebid of 4♡ offered a choice of games because a pass over 3♡ would not be forcing and a double would be penalty orientated.

West leads the six of clubs. What chance do you see here?

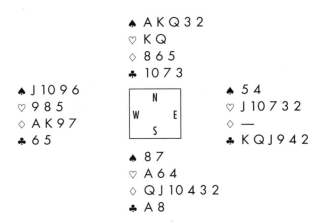

```
                    ♠ A K Q 3 2
                    ♡ K Q
                    ◇ 8 6 5
                    ♣ 10 7 3
  ♠ J 10 9 6          ┌─────────┐         ♠ 5 4
  ♡ 9 8 5             │    N    │         ♡ J 10 7 3 2
  ◇ A K 9 7           │ W     E │         ◇ —
  ♣ 6 5               │    S    │         ♣ K Q J 9 4 2
                      └─────────┘
                    ♠ 8 7
                    ♡ A 6 4
                    ◇ Q J 10 4 3 2
                    ♣ A 8
```

You are playing in 5◇ doubled after East has shown a two-suiter in hearts and clubs. West, to double 5◇, probably holds the four missing trumps. The lead is a club.

Even if you think trumps might break 3-1, you can ill afford to play them yet. After winning with the ace of clubs, you must first aim to dispose of the club loser. You do not expect the spades to break 3-3, but perhaps East will have two spades and a void in trumps and thus be unable to ruff the third round. So it turns out.

Now you know for sure that West has four trumps and, on the surface, three winners. Perhaps you can achieve a trump end-play, shortening your trumps to the same length as West's. From this point, you need West to hold a 4-3-4-2 shape. (You could also cope with 5-3-4-1 or 3-3-4-3 if East has shown up with one or three spades respectively.)

You ruff the fourth spade, cash the king-queen of hearts and ruff a club. Next, you lead the heart ace, which stands up. Now, with four cards left, you lead the queen of diamonds. If West wins, dummy's eight will become a big card. If not, you will continue with the jack and make the ten at the end. This leaves West with some explaining to do as to why it was necessary to double.

Unexpected Failure

```
          ♠ A 7 2
          ♡ Q 4
          ◊ 7 6 5
          ♣ A K Q 10 2
```

◊ 2 led

```
          N
      W       E
          S
```

```
          ♠ Q 6
          ♡ A K J 9 3
          ◊ 9 8 3
          ♣ 8 7 5
```

Dealer East
Neither vul.

WEST	NORTH	EAST	SOUTH
		1◊	1♡
pass	2♣	pass	2♡
pass	4♡	all pass	

You have agreed to play a change of suit response to an overcall as forcing for one round — a sensible treatment. Those not doing so would have to start by cuebidding opener's suit on the North hand, but they would reach the same final contract.

West starts with the two of diamonds. East cashes three top diamonds, to which all follow (West having 10-x-x), and then leads the ten of hearts. It looks easy, so consider what could possibly go wrong.

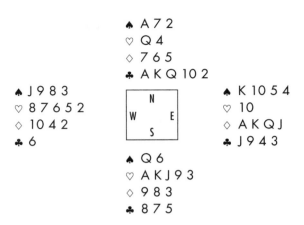

```
                    ♠ A 7 2
                    ♡ Q 4
                    ◇ 7 6 5
                    ♣ A K Q 10 2
  ♠ J 9 8 3          ┌──────────┐      ♠ K 10 5 4
  ♡ 8 7 6 5 2        │    N     │      ♡ 10
  ◇ 10 4 2           │ W     E  │      ◇ A K Q J
  ♣ 6                │    S     │      ♣ J 9 4 3
                     └──────────┘
                    ♠ Q 6
                    ♡ A K J 9 3
                    ◇ 9 8 3
                    ♣ 8 7 5
```

You, as South, play in 4♡. East, who has opened 1◇, wins three
rounds of the suit before switching to the ten of hearts.

The play looks so straightforward that you might feel
tempted to win with the queen of hearts and play a second
round. Alas, when hearts break 5-1 and clubs 4-1 you go down.
Discarding after dummy, East is not squeezed in spades and
clubs.

To your surprise, perhaps, you find that you have missed a
Vienna Coup. You had to cash the ace of spades before leaving
the dummy (i.e. straight after taking the ♡Q). This play seems all
the more tricky because the ace of spades might have served as
an entry after you had ruffed the fourth round of clubs.

The bidding provided a vital clue. East, who opened 1◇ on
a four-card suit and who would hardly lead the the ten of hearts
from 10-x-x-x, was sure to hold two clubs and probably more.
Therefore, you have to think about a squeeze in the black suits.

If your reasoning fails to impress East, you may point out that
a continuation of the thirteenth diamond would have beaten the
contract. You would have to take the force in dummy and could
not avoid the subsequent loss of a trump trick.

Three Important Cards

```
              ♠ K 10
              ♡ A 9 5 4
              ◇ J 10 8 4
              ♣ 10 9 2

                ┌─────────┐
                │    N    │
  ♠ 3 led       │ W     E │
                │    S    │
                └─────────┘

              ♠ Q 6 5
              ♡ K 3
              ◇ K Q 9 6
              ♣ A Q J 4
```

Dealer West
E–W vul.

WEST	NORTH	EAST	SOUTH
pass	pass	pass	1♣
1♠	dbl	pass	2NT
pass	3NT	all pass	

Playing a weak notrump at this vulnerability, you open 1♣. Some would prefer one diamond, but I like the style of bidding the better suit; the term 'better minor' that some use to refer to the practice of opening 1♣ with 3-3 in the minors and 1◇ with 4-4 is something of a misnomer. You intend to jump to 2NT over a simple response, showing, in traditional Acol, 17-18 balanced. North's negative double has the effect of placing the declaration in the strong (but this time wrong) hand.

West leads the three of spades. How will you play from here?

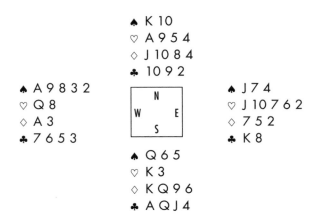

♠ K 10
♡ A 9 5 4
◇ J 10 8 4
♣ 10 9 2

♠ A 9 8 3 2
♡ Q 8
◇ A 3
♣ 7 6 5 3

♠ J 7 4
♡ J 10 7 6 2
◇ 7 5 2
♣ K 8

♠ Q 6 5
♡ K 3
◇ K Q 9 6
♣ A Q J 4

You play in 3NT after West, who passed originally, overcalled in spades. When you get a small spade lead, you should work out that the whole contract may (indeed does) depend on your first play from dummy.

It looks natural to put in the ten of spades, but you should think along these lines: to play the ten of spades from dummy will prove fatal if the spades break 5-3 (which looks to be the case from the spot card West led) and East holds the jack. If, however, you go up with the king of spades and, as expected, it wins, then you can succeed by playing on the minors if West holds the ace of diamonds and East the king of clubs.

Another way to achieve the same result is to consider the possible placing of the three missing top cards: the ♠A, the ◇A and the ♣K. Given that West passed as dealer and then produced a vulnerable overcall, and that East was unable to raise, it seems highly probable that West has two out of these three cards.

You have to assume that the club finesse succeeds whatever happens in spades. So, once you place East with the ♣K, West is more or less marked with the aces of spades and diamonds. In this case, East will never get the lead to play spades through your queen, and you are safe as long as you avoid that tempting finesse at Trick 1.

No Patience

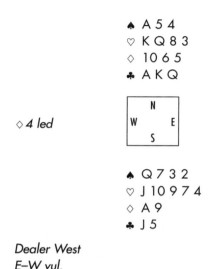

♠ A 5 4
♡ K Q 8 3
◇ 10 6 5
♣ A K Q

◇ 4 led

♠ Q 7 3 2
♡ J 10 9 7 4
◇ A 9
♣ J 5

Dealer West
E–W vul.

WEST	NORTH	EAST	SOUTH
1♠	dbl	pass	3♡
pass	4♡	all pass	

It seems marginal whether North is or is not too good for a 1NT overcall, as many play the range here as 15-18. One good reason for doubling, however, is that if the partnership belongs in 3NT, then the contract may play better from the South seat.

West leads the four of diamonds and East plays the queen. I can tell you that East holds a singleton spade, as you would expect, but the defensive hands contain no other singletons (or voids). It looks easier to make the contract than to go down!

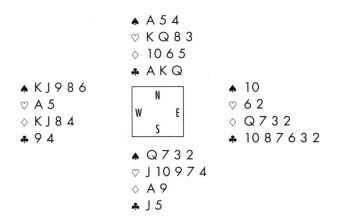

You play in four hearts after West has opened 1♠.

In a team game, both declarers won the first trick with the ace of diamonds and hastened to take a discard on the third round of clubs. You can see what happened: West ruffed the third club and led a spade to the ten and queen. When West came in with the ace of hearts, a second round of spades allowed East to ruff dummy's ace and West later scored a spade for one down.

The declarers should have foreseen this. West, who bid spades and was likely to hold ◊K-J-x-x, might well be short in clubs.

You should just tackle trumps at once. West will grab the ace and cash a diamond but, when you regain the lead, you can draw trumps, strip the minors and duck a spade. Whoever wins the trick will be endplayed and forced to give you a tenth trick.

The idea of eliminating the other suits and ducking in the key suit is a good one to remember. Say you have done that here:

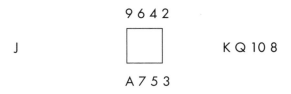

East can win two rounds of this side suit but is then stuck.

Retain a Chance

♠ 9 7 2
♡ 10 9
◇ K 10 8 7 6 5
♣ A K

◇ 4 led

```
        N
   W         E
        S
```

♠ A K
♡ A K J 7 6 5
◇ 3 2
♣ J 9 3

Dealer East
Neither vul.

WEST	NORTH	EAST	SOUTH
		1◇	2♡
pass	4♡	all pass	

In this old-fashioned sequence, both sides are playing a simple system that includes a variable notrump. Your 2♡ was strong, roughly akin to opening 1♡ and rebidding 3♡ over a simple response. You might have had a bit more shape, which may explain why partner did not angle for 3NT. In any event, the ruffing value and two useful trumps may help in 4♡.

West leads the four of diamonds (obviously a singleton). East captures dummy's eight with the nine and returns the two of hearts. You must decide whether to let this run.

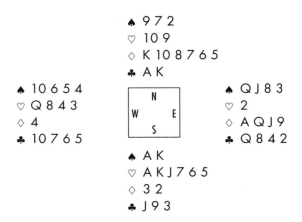

```
                    ♠ 9 7 2
                    ♡ 10 9
                    ◇ K 10 8 7 6 5
                    ♣ A K
♠ 10 6 5 4            ┌─────────┐      ♠ Q J 8 3
♡ Q 8 4 3            │    N    │      ♡ 2
◇ 4                  │ W     E │      ◇ A Q J 9
♣ 10 7 6 5          │    S    │      ♣ Q 8 4 2
                    └─────────┘
                    ♠ A K
                    ♡ A K J 7 6 5
                    ◇ 3 2
                    ♣ J 9 3
```

West leads what must be a singleton diamond against 4♡. East wins with the nine and returns a trump. Now, if you win the trick and play to ruff a club you may have two heart losers. Then again, if you play low, West may win and continue trumps, preventing the club ruff.

One way to solve the problem is to reflect that if you lose two trump tricks, you will never make the contract. By contrast, if you let the defenders play a second round of trumps, you stay in with a chance. East will come under pressure in the endgame.

The bidding provides an added reason for reading the ♡2 as a singleton. East cannot be too good for a non-vulnerable weak notrump (even with the ♡Q), yet has opened on a four-card diamond suit. A singleton heart seems a likely explanation.

So, you let West win with the queen and a heart comes back to stop the club ruff. You feel sure now that East holds the queen of clubs. Reduce your hand to a heart, a diamond and three clubs; dummy comes down to three diamonds and two clubs. If only two diamonds remain out, you can give up a diamond and establish a trick via a ruff. If there are still three lurking, East must have unguarded the queen of clubs, in which case you can cash the ace-king of clubs to set up the jack.

Unhappy Expression

$\spadesuit$ A K 4
$\heartsuit$ Q 9 5
$\diamond$ K 7 6 3
$\clubsuit$ A 6 4

```
      N
  W       E
      S
```

$\heartsuit$ J led

$\spadesuit$ J 10 8 7 6 2
$\heartsuit$ K 4
$\diamond$ J 4
$\clubsuit$ K 9 2

Dealer East
Neither vul.

WEST	NORTH	EAST	SOUTH
		1NT[1]	pass
2$\diamond$[2]	dbl[3]	2$\heartsuit$[4]	3$\spadesuit$
pass	4$\spadesuit$	all pass	

1. 12-14.
2. Transfer to hearts.
3. Showing a double of 1NT, i.e. at least 15 points.
4. Three-card heart support.

West leads the jack of hearts. You play low from dummy and so does East. How will you continue after winning with the king?

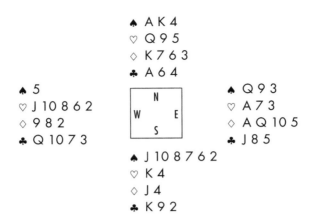

You play in 4♡ after an auction that marks East with 12-14 and three hearts. West leads the heart jack.

After winning the first round of hearts with the king, you should return a heart at once. As expected, dummy's nine draws the ace. East will probably return a third heart and you have to consider whether to discard a diamond or a club.

If East has only three diamonds, you want to throw a diamond and subsequently bring down the ace with two ruffs. However, in that case East could (assuming you have a trump loser) have beaten you with a club switch. In any event, the knowledge that East has the ace of diamonds makes it more likely that West is the one with three diamonds. (The information that hearts are 5-3 and the assumption that spades are 1-3 cancel out.)

Though you cannot guarantee success this time, the best line, which will surely work unless East has club length, is to part with a small club. Then cash the ace and king of spades and play three rounds of clubs, ruffing the third. Finally, when you exit with a spade, you will know from East's unhappy expression that the endplay has succeeded and that dummy's king of diamonds will provide your tenth trick.

Coup de Belladonna

♠ 10 4
♡ 8
◇ A 8 6 5
♣ K 10 8 5 4 3

◇ *10 led*

♠ A K 2
♡ K 10 5 4
◇ K Q J 4
♣ Q 7

Dealer West
Both vul.

WEST	NORTH	EAST	SOUTH
2◇[1]	pass	2♡[2]	2NT
pass[3]	3NT	all pass	

1. Multi: a weak two in a major or various strong hands.
2. To play, facing a weak two in hearts.
3. A weak two in one of the majors.

With support for hearts, East would bid 2♠ rather than 2♡, so you infer that West's suit is hearts.

West's lead of the ◇10 runs to the king. You lead the ♣Q, which holds, and a second club goes to the nine, ten and jack. Back comes the ♡9, covered by the ten and jack. West exits with a diamond and all follow. How would you play now?

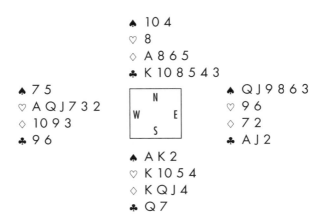

```
              ♠ 10 4
              ♡ 8
              ◇ A 8 6 5
              ♣ K 10 8 5 4 3
♠ 7 5                              ♠ Q J 9 8 6 3
♡ A Q J 7 3 2      N              ♡ 9 6
◇ 10 9 3        W     E           ◇ 7 2
♣ 9 6             S               ♣ A J 2
              ♠ A K 2
              ♡ K 10 5 4
              ◇ K Q J 4
              ♣ Q 7
```

This is a *coup de Belladonna,* originally played in a tournament in Sicily, an island of which I have fond memories. Jose Le Dentu reported it in the French magazine *Le Bridgeur*.

West, who opened with a 'Multi' and subsequently disclosed a hand with around 6-10 points and a six-card heart suit, led a diamond against 3NT. Winning in hand, the original declarer, Giorgio Belladonna, played queen and another club. East won the second club with the jack and led the nine of hearts, covered by the ten and jack. West then committed a slight error, continuing passively with a diamond to the queen (rather than attacking declarer's entries with a spade switch).

It is clear that if declarer now enters dummy with a diamond and plays a club, the opponents will have enough tricks to beat the contract — two clubs and three hearts. Giorgio Belladonna's solution was to lead a small heart. If East wins this trick, West becomes an onlooker and declarer can clear the clubs. West therefore won the trick with the queen and cashed the ace of hearts — a fourth trick for the defenders.

Belladonna won the diamond return in hand, cashed the king of hearts and went to dummy with a fourth round of diamonds. This caught East, who was down to ♠Q-J-9 and the ♣A, in a simple squeeze. Bravo!

Timely Loss

```
        ♠ A 6 5
        ♡ K
        ◇ K J 4
        ♣ 10 8 7 6 5 2
```

♣A led

```
        N
    W       E
        S
```

```
        ♠ K Q J 8 4 2
        ♡ 7 6 5 4
        ◇ A 7
        ♣ Q
```

Dealer West
Neither vul.

WEST	NORTH	EAST	SOUTH
1NT[1]	pass	2♡	2♠
3♡	3♠	pass	4♠
all pass			

1. 12-14.

Your opponents are not playing transfers and news of their heart fit improves the look of your hand. West leads the ace of clubs (from ace-king) and shifts to a trump. You win in dummy and ruff a club, all following. When you lead a heart, West takes the ace and leads a second spade; again all follow.

Apart, perhaps, from missing an opening trump lead, West has done well to prevent you from ruffing two hearts. If East has the ◇Q and no more clubs, you are a trick short. What is your plan?

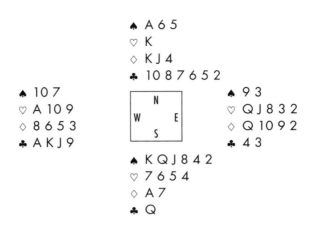

```
              ♠ A 6 5
              ♡ K
              ◇ K J 4
              ♣ 10 8 7 6 5 2
  ♠ 10 7                          ♠ 9 3
  ♡ A 10 9        N               ♡ Q J 8 3 2
  ◇ 8 6 5 3    W     E            ◇ Q 10 9 2
  ♣ A K J 9       S               ♣ 4 3
              ♠ K Q J 8 4 2
              ♡ 7 6 5 4
              ◇ A 7
              ♣ Q
```

You play in 4♠ after West has opened with a weak notrump and raised East's hearts.

So far the play has gone ♣A, ♠A, club ruff, heart to the ace, and another trump. Your prospects are excellent, even if West still has the clubs well guarded and regardless of who has the ◇Q. You envisage a squeeze with West protecting clubs, East protecting hearts and neither able to keep the diamonds.

After winning the second round of trumps in hand, duck the next round of hearts, discarding a club from dummy, obviously. Having done this, you win West's diamond return with the ace, ruff the third round of hearts in dummy, ruff a club to hand and finish the trumps. If, as will probably happen, West retains a club, you will throw dummy's ♣10 on the last trump to keep your ◇K-J.

Do you see how the defenders can beat the contract if you ruff a heart prematurely? East, for the last five tricks, keeps three diamonds as well as the queen and eight of hearts. You cannot give up a heart, as East can overtake West's ten with the queen and cash the eight. If, instead, you cash your last trump, East unblocks the ♡Q to avoid being endplayed. Alternatively, if you cross to the ◇K and ruff a club, East bares the ◇Q and scores two hearts at the end.

Surprise Target

```
         ♠ A Q 5 2
         ♡ Q 5
         ♢ Q 7 5 4
         ♣ A 8 2
```

```
            ┌─────────┐
            │    N    │
♠6 led      │ W     E │
            │    S    │
            └─────────┘
```

```
         ♠ 8 3
         ♡ A K J 10 9 3
         ♢ A K 10 2
         ♣ 7
```

Dealer East
Neither vul.

WEST	NORTH	EAST	SOUTH
		2♠	4♡
pass	6♡	all pass	

East's opening bid was a weak two, implying a six-card spade suit and somewhere between a good 5 points and a moderate 10. West leads the six of spades.

All will turn out well if diamonds break 3-2 or if, unexpectedly, East has four, but suppose West has ◇J-x-x-x. What can you do about that?

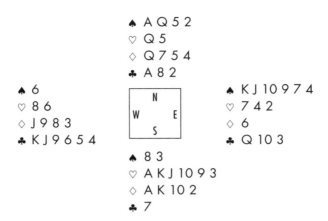

```
                    ♠ A Q 5 2
                    ♡ Q 5
                    ◇ Q 7 5 4
                    ♣ A 8 2
  ♠ 6                    N          ♠ K J 10 9 7 4
  ♡ 8 6             W          E    ♡ 7 4 2
  ◇ J 9 8 3              S          ◇ 6
  ♣ K J 9 6 5 4                     ♣ Q 10 3
                    ♠ 8 3
                    ♡ A K J 10 9 3
                    ◇ A K 10 2
                    ♣ 7
```

You are in 6♡ and West leads a spade. You must win this, since East, who opened a weak two in spades, is marked with six cards in the suit. You have six sure trump tricks and two aces to make, so a problem will arise only if West holds four diamonds to the jack. There might then be faint chances of a squeeze (or a throw-in) against this defender, but this would depend on East's inability to guard the third round of clubs. It seems a better chance to put East in the hot seat in a way that may not appear obvious at first.

First, cash the ace of clubs. Then ruff two clubs in hand (using the queen of hearts as a re-entry) and draw trumps, discarding a diamond from dummy. You observe that East, who has followed to three rounds of clubs, cannot possibly hold ◇J-x-x-x, and now you cash the ace and king of diamonds. When you find the suit breaking 4-1 (indeed you already knew this), you simply duck a spade. East, who has only spades left, can do no better than to win and exit with the king. Ruffing this, you cross to dummy with a diamond and cash the spade queen. Now you see why it was essential to keep the queen of diamonds as an entry to the table!

An equivalent line of play is to cash only one high diamond before your spade exit. If East has another diamond, the suit is breaking. If not, he is endplayed as before.

Somewhat Unusual

```
         ♠ J 9 4
         ♡ A J 10 5
         ◇ A K 6
         ♣ A K 7
```

♠5 led

```
        ┌─────────┐
        │    N    │
        │ W     E │
        │    S    │
        └─────────┘
```

```
         ♠ A K Q 10 8 6 2
         ♡ —
         ◇ 7 4 2
         ♣ 6 4 3
```

Dealer East
Neither vul.

WEST	NORTH	EAST	SOUTH
		2♡	3♠
pass	5NT	pass	6NT
pass	7♠	all pass	

The 6NT reply to the 5NT trump inquiry showed the top three spades — at least that is what South said afterwards. East's bid is weak, of course.

West leads a trump — customary against a grand slam — and East follows. You can see twelve very fine winners: seven solid trumps, two ace-kings and the ace of hearts. You surely need a squeeze, but the snag is that even if West has a five-card minor, the two singly-guarded menaces will be wrongly placed for a double squeeze. Can the knowledge that West has three hearts and East six help in some way?

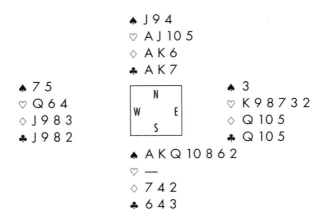

You have a chance if the ♡K and ♡Q lie in opposite hands, as then West cannot throw a heart without exposing East to a ruffing finesse. Five rounds of spades will leave each defender guarding one minor in a position something like this:

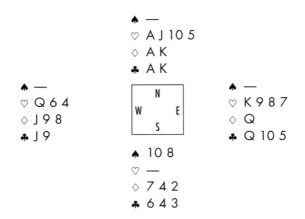

Cashing the ◇A-K now catches East in a trump squeeze: a club discard would set up your six whilst a heart discard would let you ruff out the suit. The position is somewhat unusual, but it shows what you can do with a long suit and excellent top cards.

Only Nine

```
        ♠ 5 4
        ♡ K Q 9 8 6
        ◇ A J 9 4 2
        ♣ 2
```

```
              N
♠Q led    W       E
              S
```

```
        ♠ A 10 8 2
        ♡ A 7 2
        ◇ 7
        ♣ J 10 8 6 5
```

Dealer West
Neither vul.

WEST	NORTH	EAST	SOUTH
1NT[1]	2♣[2]	pass	3♡[3]
pass	4♡	all pass	

1. 12-14.
2. Asptro: hearts and another, 5-4/4-5 at least in the suits.
3. A little aggressive with only three-card support.

West leads the queen of spades, which you win with your ace.
You lead the jack of clubs from hand and West wins the queen
before switching to the four of hearts. East plays the ten and you
win with the ♡A. Which way will you go for ten tricks?

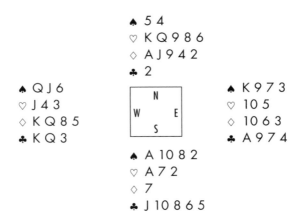

```
                    ♠ 5 4
                    ♡ K Q 9 8 6
                    ◇ A J 9 4 2
                    ♣ 2
  ♠ Q J 6              ┌─────────┐        ♠ K 9 7 3
  ♡ J 4 3             │    N     │        ♡ 10 5
  ◇ K Q 8 5          │ W     E  │        ◇ 10 6 3
  ♣ K Q 3            │    S     │        ♣ A 9 7 4
                      └─────────┘
                    ♠ A 10 8 2
                    ♡ A 7 2
                    ◇ 7
                    ♣ J 10 8 6 5
```

West, who has shown a balanced hand with 12-14 points, leads the queen of spades against 4♡. You win and advance the jack of clubs. When West wins and returns a trump, a few frustrating attempts at projecting the play will convince you that a simple crossruff will produce only nine tricks. You might reach a position in which you have set up a long card in one of the minors, but you will not have any trumps left in either hand to be able to enjoy it.

So, you have to find extra tricks in diamonds. Lead the seven and play the jack from dummy if West plays low. This wins if West holds any of K-10-x, Q-10-x, K-Q-x or K-Q-x-x.

West may try inserting the king or queen on the first round of diamonds. In this case, you win with the ace and return the jack, discarding a club from hand. West may win, cash the jack of spades and lead a trump, but you are in control. You can ruff a diamond, bring down the ten and make game by way of one spade, five hearts, the ace of diamonds, a diamond ruff and two long diamonds. This line will win against three of the four West holdings noted above, losing only to K-Q-x (East will still have 10-8 over dummy's 9).

The trap to avoid is finessing the nine of diamonds if you get the chance — nobody would duck with K-Q-10-x and you cannot succeed anyway if West has K-10-x-x or Q-10-x-x.

Either Way

```
        ♠ J 3
        ♡ J 8 6 2
        ◇ 10 7 5 3
        ♣ A 10 6
```

```
            N
        W       E
            S
```

♡ A led

```
        ♠ A K Q 10 9 6
        ♡ 7
        ◇ A K Q
        ♣ K 9 4
```

Dealer West
Both vul.

WEST	NORTH	EAST	SOUTH
1♡	pass	pass	2♡
pass	3◇	pass	4♠
pass	5♣	pass	6♠
all pass			

Two hearts, in the rubber bridge style, indicates a very strong
hand. North's 5♣, after your jump to 4♠, is surely a cuebid and
an imaginative slam try.

West begins with two top hearts, East playing the four and
five. Ruffing the second heart, you need to justify your side's
bold bidding. Can you do it if East holds ◇J-x-x-x? Can you also
handle that holding with West? (Trumps are 3-2.)

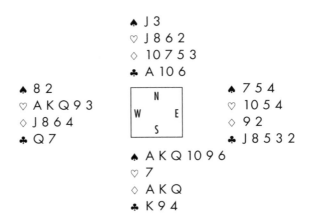

In 6♠, you ruff the second heart, cash the ♠A, cross to the ♠J and
ruff a heart. Then, on the next trump, dummy *unblocks* the ♣10.
You cash the ◊A-K-Q and find that West has four diamonds.
There would have been a double squeeze if East had the diamonds. As it is, you arrive at this ending (a guard squeeze):

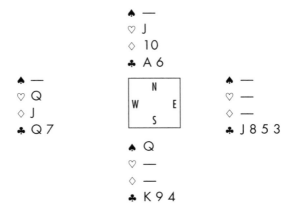

On the last spade, West must throw a club. When the queen then
appears as you cross to the ♣A you can be sure a finesse of the
♣9 will win, because you know West's last two cards.

Clean Sheet

```
        ♠ J 6 5 2
        ♡ K 6 3 2
        ◇ K Q 9
        ♣ 4 3
```

```
              N
            W   E
              S
```

♣A led

```
        ♠ K 7 3
        ♡ A 5 4
        ◇ A J 10 7 6 4 3
        ♣ —
```

Dealer West
E–W vul.

WEST	NORTH	EAST	SOUTH
1♠	pass	2♣	2◇
4♣	4◇	5♣	5◇
all pass			

After an entirely natural sequence from the rubber bridge table, you manage to buy the contract by virtue of possessing the higher-ranking trump suit. (The vulnerability may also have worked to your advantage.)

West leads the ace of clubs. There seem to be three certain losers: two spades and a heart. What can you do about them?

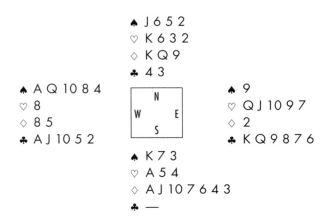

♠ J 6 5 2
♡ K 6 3 2
◇ K Q 9
♣ 4 3

♠ A Q 10 8 4
♡ 8
◇ 8 5
♣ A J 10 5 2

♠ 9
♡ Q J 10 9 7
◇ 2
♣ K Q 9 8 7 6

♠ K 7 3
♡ A 5 4
◇ A J 10 7 6 4 3
♣ —

After West has opened 1♠ and both opponents have bid clubs vigorously, you play in 5◇ on the lead of the ace of clubs. You would make your name if word got around that you got this one right at the table.

If East is 1-3-3-6 or 1-3-2-7 with a singleton queen of spades, you might set up a long heart and lose just one trick in each major, but this seems rather against the odds. Taking advantage of the defenders' likely communication difficulties represents a better bet. You know that East is short in spades and West, who has length in both black suits, figures to be short in hearts.

Ruff the opening lead and draw trumps. Then play a heart to the king, ruff a club, and cash the ace of hearts. You probably expected a 2-4 heart split but it comes as no great surprise when West shows out. Now lead a small spade. If West takes the queen, any return will be helpful, either giving you a second spade trick or a ruff and discard. In practice, West plays low, so dummy's jack wins and you exit with a heart. East makes two heart tricks (you throw a spade on the fourth round) and then has to concede a ruff and discard. Somewhat remarkably, you have not lost a single trick in spades!

A Little Leeway

```
        ♠ 10 5
        ♡ K Q
        ◇ Q 9 7 5 4
        ♣ A K 7 4
```

```
        N
    W       E
        S
```

♠K led

```
        ♠ A J 8
        ♡ A 10 5 2
        ◇ A K 4
        ♣ J 8 3
```

Dealer West
Neither vul.

WEST	NORTH	EAST	SOUTH
3♠	pass	pass	3NT
pass	4NT	pass	5NT
pass	6NT	all pass	

The range for a 3NT overcall of a three-level preempt extends a long way, possibly from as little as 15 points to a maximum of 22. Accordingly, North makes a quantitative raise and you, not completely minimum, raise the level one more; this proves sufficient to encourage North to go on to the slam.

West leads the king of spades. No problem will arise if the diamonds behave, but do you expect them to behave in this book?

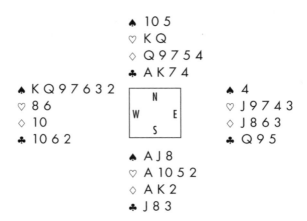

```
                    ♠ 10 5
                    ♡ K Q
                    ◇ Q 9 7 5 4
                    ♣ A K 7 4
♠ K Q 9 7 6 3 2    ┌──────────┐    ♠ 4
♡ 8 6              │    N     │    ♡ J 9 7 4 3
◇ 10              │ W      E │    ◇ J 8 6 3
♣ 10 6 2          │    S     │    ♣ Q 9 5
                   └──────────┘
                    ♠ A J 8
                    ♡ A 10 5 2
                    ◇ A K 2
                    ♣ J 8 3
```

You are in 6NT and West, who opened 3♠, leads the king of
spades. Since you may well need a second trick in spades even
if the diamonds break evenly, you win and return the ♠8.

We will assume for the moment that West takes the queen
and exits with a club. You win in dummy and your best play is
to cash the ♡K-Q and a second club before testing the diamonds.
Neither the queen of clubs nor the jack of hearts has dropped and
now you find that West shows out on the second round of diamonds. Fortunately, there is no need to panic. East may be protecting three suits and find the pressure unbearable when you
cash the jack of spades, throwing a club from dummy. A diamond discard would give you two tricks straight away and, if
East discards the queen of clubs or bares the jack of hearts, you
will have a new winner with which to apply further pressure.

West may decline to take the queen of spades when you play
the suit straight back. In some circumstances, this would be a
winning tactic. You can overcome it here by cashing two hearts
and playing four rounds of diamonds, throwing a spade from
hand. Then you will have a long diamond set up and, holding
the ♡J and ♣Q, East cannot exit safely in either hearts or clubs.

Profit and Loss

```
        ♠ —
        ♡ Q 5 3 2
        ◇ A Q 7 6 2
        ♣ 9 6 3 2

                  N
♣K led        W       E
                  S


        ♠ K J
        ♡ A K J 10 6
        ◇ K 5 3
        ♣ A J 4
```

Dealer South
E–W vul.

WEST	NORTH	EAST	SOUTH
			1♡
4♠	5♡	pass	6♡
all pass			

You might have opened 2NT, but it is probably just as well that you chose not to, as you might have missed the heart fit. West leads the king of clubs against your slam.

The bidding forewarns of bad breaks. If hearts split 3-1 and diamonds 4-1, you cannot conveniently take two spade ruffs, draw trumps and make four tricks in diamonds. How will you tackle the play?

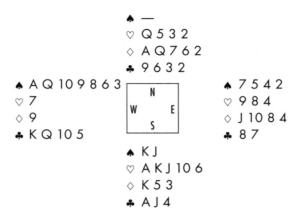

West, who is vulnerable and has overcalled with 4♠, leads the king of clubs against your contract of 6♡.

You take the ♣A and cash the ♡A-K. You try two rounds of diamonds before playing the ◇Q and ruffing a diamond. You cross to the ♡Q and throw a club on the fifth diamond. Then a club to the jack and queen leaves West on play in this position:

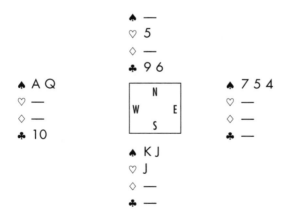

It was unnecessary, you see, to ruff two spades early on. You had to profit from the useful holdings in the black suits.

Form a Picture

```
        ♠ Q
        ♡ K 8 2
        ◇ K Q 8 3
        ♣ 8 7 5 4 3

              ┌─────────┐
              │    N    │
♣ K led       │ W     E │
              │    S    │
              └─────────┘

        ♠ A 5 2
        ♡ A J 10 7 4 3
        ◇ A 5 2
        ♣ J
```

Dealer South
Both vul.

WEST	NORTH	EAST	SOUTH
			1♡
2♡	4♡	4♠	6♡
all pass			

West's 2♡ indicated spades and a minor, with at least five cards
in each. You and partner were playing five-card majors, but even
so, North's 4♡ appears to be an overbid; a cuebid of 2♠ to show
a raise to 3♡ based on some high cards would have been sufficient. Your leap to the slam was also imaginative; presuming
that the majors would play without loss was reasonable, but
North might have had weaker diamonds.

West leads the king of clubs and East overtakes with the ace
before switching to a heart. You play the ten, which holds the
trick, West dropping the nine. Can you see a way home now?

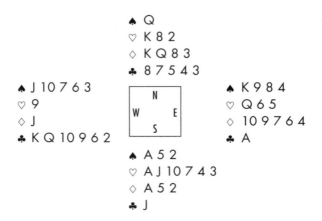

You play in 6♡ after West has made a two-suited overcall, showing spades and a minor, and East has competed to 4♠. East overtakes West's king of clubs lead with the ace and switches to a trump, which your ten wins.

The play to the first two tricks, together with the bidding, makes it likely that West started with five spades and six clubs. If so, then given that everyone followed to the first round of trumps and that the defenders have not taken a diamond ruff, you can read West for a 5-1-1-6 distribution.

You do best to play diamonds at once and the appearance of West's jack seems to confirm your suspicion. The danger now is that ruffing two spades in dummy will give you a trump loser.

You plan for a trump coup, however. Having won the first diamond trick with the queen, ruff a club, cash the ace of spades, take a spade ruff, and ruff another club. To keep the diamonds guarded, East will have thrown one spade and one diamond. You continue with the ace and king of diamonds, ruff the fourth round in hand, and then ruff a spade with the king of hearts. All this hard work now bears fruit, as you have the lead in dummy with the ♡A-J in your hand sitting pretty over East's Q-x.

```
          ♠ 7 5 3 2
          ♡ J 8
          ◇ K 7 4
          ♣ 6 5 4 2

                  ┌─────────┐
                  │    N    │
  ♣A led          │ W     E │
                  │    S    │
                  └─────────┘

          ♠ A K
          ♡ K Q 10 9 5
          ◇ A Q 5 3
          ♣ 8 3
```

Dealer West
Both vul.

WEST	NORTH	EAST	SOUTH
2♣	pass	pass	dbl
pass	2♠	pass	3♡
all pass			

East-West are playing Precision, in which a 2♣ opening signifies a fair suit of clubs and not more than about 15 points. On their system, it should show either six or more clubs or at least five clubs plus a four-card major.

West begins with the three top clubs. East follows twice and discards a spade on the third round, which you ruff. How do you play from here?

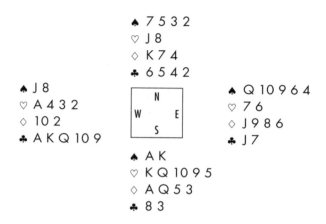

```
              ♠ 7 5 3 2
              ♡ J 8
              ◇ K 7 4
              ♣ 6 5 4 2
♠ J 8                          ♠ Q 10 9 6 4
♡ A 4 3 2         N            ♡ 7 6
◇ 10 2      W         E        ◇ J 9 8 6
♣ A K Q 10 9      S            ♣ J 7
              ♠ A K
              ♡ K Q 10 9 5
              ◇ A Q 5 3
              ♣ 8 3
```

You play in 3♡ after West opened with a natural but limited two clubs. All follow to two rounds of clubs and you ruff the third round, East discarding a spade. If this discard comes from a long suit, as seems likely, then West, who should systemically hold a four-card major, probably has four hearts to the ace. In this case, playing on trumps will put the contract in danger, because West will force you again in clubs.

You cannot cater for every eventuality, but the right line is to start by taking two rounds of spades. When all follow, cash the ◇A-K and give up a diamond. Now, if the defenders play two rounds of trumps, you will be in control, able to draw the last two trumps and cash the queen of diamonds. If they do not play two rounds of trumps, dummy's ♡J-8 will take care of the fourth diamond.

You may be wondering why I suggest cashing the two top spades early. Well, East might just hold ♡A-x, and if West discards from a doubleton spade on the third round of diamonds, then you will run into a ruff and lose a diamond as well.

Of course, to play even one round of trumps would prove fatal. Then, when you ducked the diamond, the defenders could draw dummy's remaining trump and force you with a club.

```
            ♠ K 8 7
            ♡ K 8 6 2
            ◇ K 7 2
            ♣ 6 5 3
```

```
                    ┌───────────┐
                    │     N     │
♠ J led             │ W       E │
                    │     S     │
                    └───────────┘
```

```
            ♠ —
            ♡ J 4
            ◇ A Q 8 6 3
            ♣ A K Q J 10 2
```

Dealer East
E–W vul.

WEST	NORTH	EAST	SOUTH
		1♠	2NT
pass	3◇	pass	4♣
pass	5♣	all pass	

Using a 2NT overcall to show the lowest two unbid suits has become almost universal. The one area in which its treatment varies is whether it can cover intermediate hands. Some reserve its use for weak hands, or for strong hands like this one, where you know you can go higher if partner makes a minimum bid.

West leads the jack of spades and you ruff. You try two rounds of trumps and West discards a spade on the second round. The play may prove awkward now if East, who has the outstanding trump, holds the ace of hearts, as seems more or less certain, together with a singleton diamond. What can you do?

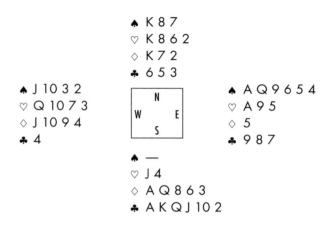

♠ K 8 7
♡ K 8 6 2
◇ K 7 2
♣ 6 5 3

♠ J 10 3 2
♡ Q 10 7 3
◇ J 10 9 4
♣ 4

N
W E
S

♠ A Q 9 6 5 4
♡ A 9 5
◇ 5
♣ 9 8 7

♠ —
♡ J 4
◇ A Q 8 6 3
♣ A K Q J 10 2

Playing in 5♣ after an opening bid of 1♠ by East, you ruff the
spade lead. When you draw two rounds of trumps, West shows
out. East is likely to hold six spades (or West, with five-card support and a singleton, would have raised) and may well hold a singleton diamond. In any case, unless diamonds break unkindly,
you have eleven easy tricks.

Firstly, you need to see that you can safely continue with the
ace and queen of diamonds. East, upon ruffing, would have to
lead from an ace and there would be a trump in dummy to deal
with the fourth diamond.

If East sees this and declines to ruff, you lead a third round
of diamonds to the king. For the reason just discussed, this
holds. Now you ruff a spade and lead a fourth round of diamonds, discarding dummy's third and last spade.

Up until this point, the spotlight has fallen on East but now
West moves into the hot seat. A spade lead would concede a ruff
and discard, so West tries a small heart. Knowing East has the
ace, and hoping West has the queen, you let this run.

You are right; this is probably the trickiest deal in the book so
far, even though you can determine the lie of the cards fairly
well.

High Pressure

```
      ♠ 4 3
      ♡ J 2
      ◇ A Q 10 7 3
      ♣ K 7 4 3
```

```
          N
      W       E
          S
```

♠ 6 led

```
      ♠ A 9 8 7
      ♡ K Q 10 6
      ◇ K 6
      ♣ A 5 2
```

Dealer East
Both vul.

WEST	NORTH	EAST	SOUTH
		1♠	1NT
pass	3NT	all pass	

Certain players in your position would have mistakenly doubled
1♠ (how would they cope with 2◇ from North?). This time the
final contract would have been the same because North would
have bid 3◇.

West leads the six of spades to East's ten. Even if you make
five tricks in diamonds, you will be a trick short. Even someone
playing five-card majors might decide to fudge a bit and open one
spade on K-Q-J-10 (when you could afford to knock out the ace
of hearts) but you would prefer a better chance. What do you
suggest?

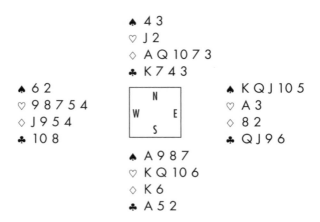

Playing in 3NT, you do not appear well placed after a spade lead on which East, who opened 1♠, played the ten. Almost certainly East holds more than four spades, but gaining a sure count on the suit may prove helpful, so it costs nothing to hold off a couple of rounds. All follow to the second spade and, when you win the third round, West discards a heart and dummy a club.

Assuming that West cannot really hold the ace of hearts on the bidding, the only chance for this contract will come if East has to protect three suits and cannot discard conveniently on the long diamonds. This means that you must place East with four (or more) clubs and the ace of hearts in addition to five spades.

There is no certainty, but on balance you should play for the diamonds to split 4-2 and finesse the ten on the second round. (To make the contract with diamonds 3-3, East's ♡A would have to be singleton, and J-x-x-x with West is twice as likely as x-x-x-x.) East can discard a club and a heart on this trick and the next one, but the fifth diamond proves too much. Discarding the ace of hearts is obviously out, whilst a spade discard would allow you to knock out the ace of hearts; if East discards another club on the fifth diamond, you will actually make your contract without benefit of a single heart trick.

Pessimistic View

```
        ♠ 6 5
        ♡ 10 6 5
        ◇ Q 7 6 5
        ♣ A K 9 3
```

```
            ┌─────────┐
            │    N    │
♠ K led     │ W     E │
            │    S    │
            └─────────┘
```

```
        ♠ A
        ♡ A K 9 7 4 2
        ◇ A K 10 2
        ♣ 8 2
```

Dealer South
Both vul.

WEST	NORTH	EAST	SOUTH
			2♡
4♠	5♡	pass	6♡
all pass			

You have opened with an Acol (strong) two-bid. North has taken
what may turn out to be a good view in going to 5♡ in preference
to doubling 4♠. Although strong two-bids have been going out of
fashion even on this side of the 'pond', you have to admit that it
would have proven difficult to reach the slam if you had opened
1♡.

West leads the king of spades and East plays the nine. You
can take the first spade quickly if you like, but I suggest you give
a good deal of thought to the problem before deciding what to do
next.

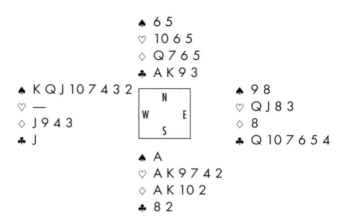

You play in 6♡. West, who is vulnerable and has overcalled 4♠, leads the king of spades, on which East plays the nine.

You might take one look here and think: 'I can afford to lay down the ace of hearts because even if West is void I shall lose only one trump trick.' That is true as far as it goes, but you need to consider another point: might you lose a diamond trick?

Since, as we have discussed, the hearts present no serious problem, you should reflect that only one thing will endanger the contract, namely a holding of ◇J-x-x-x with West. It may not seem very probable, but you cannot ignore the possibility. In this case, you will need to play the trumps without loss.

East would hardly play the nine from 9-x-x, so the spades are probably 8-2. With seven clubs but only four trumps missing, West is more likely to be 8-0-4-1 than 8-1-4-0. This makes it right to cross to dummy in clubs and run the ♡10. If this loses to the jack or queen (and West has a club), the diamonds will break reasonably and you will make the rest. In practice, East covers and you use dummy's remaining entries to finesse twice more.

On this instructive deal, you needed to think: 'What is the worst that can happen?' and consider what would follow from that.

follow the Trail

```
          ♠ A Q 4
          ♡ 9 7 5
          ◇ A Q 4 2
          ♣ 10 5 3

                    N
    ♣ K led      W     E
                    S

          ♠ 8 7 6 3
          ♡ A K Q 6 4
          ◇ J 10 6 3
          ♣ —
```

Dealer East
Neither vul.

WEST	NORTH	EAST	SOUTH
		1NT[1]	2♡
3♣	4♡	all pass	

1. 12-14.

In this rubber bridge sequence, West's 3♣ is purely competitive. In match play, many pairs treat a direct 3♣ as forcing and use a Lebensohl 2NT bid to indicate a hand that merely wishes to compete (or they might use transfers, as we saw earlier). In addition, North-South would probably have a better way to describe the South hand than a simple 2♡.

West leads the king of clubs (from K-Q) and you ruff. How will you set about making this contract?

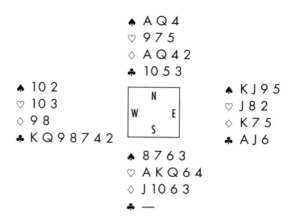

```
                        ♠ A Q 4
                        ♡ 9 7 5
                        ◇ A Q 4 2
                        ♣ 10 5 3
   ♠ 10 2                              ♠ K J 9 5
   ♡ 10 3          ┌──── N ────┐       ♡ J 8 2
   ◇ 9 8           W          E        ◇ K 7 5
   ♣ K Q 9 8 7 4 2 └──── S ────┘       ♣ A J 6
                        ♠ 8 7 6 3
                        ♡ A K Q 6 4
                        ◇ J 10 6 3
                        ♣ —
```

After West has immediately turned up with the ♣K-Q, you can guarantee that East, who opened a weak 1NT, holds the king of diamonds and the king of spades. What are your losers?

Even ignoring the fourth spade, you have three losers in the side suits. If the defenders plug away at clubs every time they gain the lead, you will have to ruff three times; therefore, unless you find the J-10 doubleton, you will lose a trump trick as well.

What is the answer? Well, hope for a 7-3 club split and let them play their game. After ruffing the first club, cash one heart, then play the six of diamonds to the queen and king. East may lead another club, but a trump is better, which we assume is what you get. You win this trump and lead the ten of diamonds to the ace. Then you ruff a second club, play a spade to the ace, and ruff dummy's third club with your last trump, the queen.

After cashing the ◇J, you lead the cleverly preserved three of diamonds to the four in dummy. East faces the unhappy choice of ruffing this, and being endplayed at once, or of waiting to be thrown in on the third round of trumps. Either way a lead around to dummy's ♠Q gives you a tenth trick. This was an unusual dummy reversal in that you created a trump loser by ruffing but the trick came back on an elimination play.

```
            ♠ 10 8 6 5
            ♡ 6
            ◇ A Q J 2
            ♣ Q 8 6 5
                  ┌─────────┐
                  │    N    │
  ♣2 led          │ W     E │
                  │    S    │
                  └─────────┘
            ♠ 2
            ♡ A K Q J 9 7 2
            ◇ 7 3
            ♣ K 7 4
```

Dealer North
Both vul.

WEST	NORTH	EAST	SOUTH
	pass	1♣	4♡
all pass			

East-West are playing a strong notrump, so East's 1♣ could be made on only a three-card suit. Your jump to 4♡ looks fine. Facing a passed partner there was no point in taking the auction slowly. Doing so might have allowed the opponents to get together in spades if they had a fit.

West leads the ♣2. East puts up the ten on the first trick and you naturally win with the king. How should you plan the play?

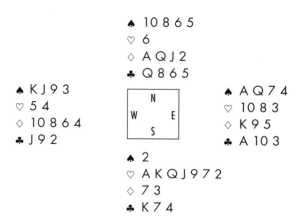

♠ 10 8 6 5
♡ 6
◇ A Q J 2
♣ Q 8 6 5

♠ K J 9 3
♡ 5 4
◇ 10 8 6 4
♣ J 9 2

♠ A Q 7 4
♡ 10 8 3
◇ K 9 5
♣ A 10 3

♠ 2
♡ A K Q J 9 7 2
◇ 7 3
♣ K 7 4

As South, you play in 4♡ after East has opened 1♣. West leads the ♣2 to East's ten and your king.

When you saw West's lead, you feared that the defenders would score the first four tricks with two black aces and two club ruffs. Evidently, their clubs are 3-3 rather than 1-5.

You can draw trumps in three rounds and safely discard two spades from dummy. How should you continue?

It seems unlikely West has underled the ♣A, so suppose you try the diamond finesse. East takes the king and, counting you for ten tricks (seven trumps, a club and two diamonds), leads a small spade. West wins and reverts to clubs.

You could play clubs instead of diamonds, but it comes to the same thing. If you duck the second round of clubs (as you would if there was a chance East might hold A-x), West gets in to make the killing diamond switch. You do better to force East to win the first round of clubs, but West can get in if East underleads the ace of spades.

The solution is simple. After drawing trumps, you lead a spade to sever the link between the defenders. West does best to win and play a club, but dummy's queen covers and East cannot hurt you. After ruffing the next spade you will be able to set up a long club and make ten tricks.

```
          ♠ A K 10 3
          ♡ 9 3
          ◇ 6 5 4
          ♣ 6 4 3 2
```

```
            ┌─────────┐
            │    N    │
♡ Q led     │ W     E │
            │    S    │
            └─────────┘
```

```
          ♠ Q 9 6 5 4 2
          ♡ A 8
          ◇ K 8 7
          ♣ A 10
```

Dealer South
E–W vul.

WEST	NORTH	EAST	SOUTH
			1♠
dbl	3♠	all pass	

As is standard these days, North's jump raise indicates a hand with four-card spade support but only the values to bid 2♠ without the double. This makes it difficult for the fourth player to come in. The strategy seems to have worked well since, as the doubler most likely has the diamond ace, it looks like you would need a club ruff to defeat 4♡.

In your contract, how do you plan to avoid the loss of three diamonds, a heart and a club?

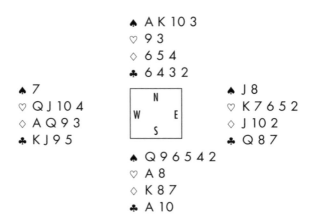

Against your 3♠, West, who doubled 1♠ for takeout, leads the queen of hearts.

Once you place East with the king of hearts, it becomes highly likely that West holds the ace of diamonds. If this card is doubleton, West has made a weird takeout double. Surely an elimination offers the best chance to deal with the ◊A offside.

If the double was on a 2-4-4-3, 1-4-5-3 shape or similar, you are in trouble. For a throw-in to work you surely need East not to have four clubs. First, you need to remove West's exit cards without allowing East to make a killing diamond switch.

Duck the opening lead (or win if East overtakes, hoping that West has the ten) and win the trump shift in dummy (nothing else is better defensively). Then play a club to the ten (East cannot gain by playing the queen) and take the heart return. Next, you unblock the ♣A, go across with a trump and ruff a club. Return to dummy with a trump and play a fourth club. East shows out and you discard a diamond to endplay West, who must either set up your ◊K or concede a ruff and discard.

As the cards lie, it takes an initial trump lead to defeat the contract. You could not then arrange to make avoidance plays in hearts and clubs and play two further rounds of clubs.

Drastic Action

```
        ♠ 10 5 4
        ♡ 9 5
        ◇ 9 7 5 4 2
        ♣ K 9 4
```

♣J led

```
          ┌─────┐
          │  N  │
        W │     │ E  ·
          │  S  │
          └─────┘
```

```
        ♠ A K 8 7 3
        ♡ A K Q J 10
        ◇ Q 8 3
        ♣ —
```

Dealer East
Both vul.

WEST	NORTH	EAST	SOUTH
		pass	1♣[1]
pass	1◇[2]	pass	1♠
pass	2♠	pass	4♠
all pass			

1. Precision, 16+ and almost any shape.
2. 0-7 and almost any shape.

Personally, I regret the recent decline in the popularity of strong club systems. They and their advocates have much to offer to the game, and I appreciate diversity. Having already given a negative, North could pass 1♠, but with three trumps, a doubleton and a king, the raise seems fine.

What chances can you see to prevent the loss of three diamonds as well as a spade?

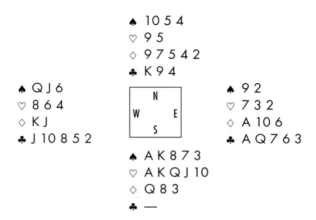

```
                    ♠ 10 5 4
                    ♡ 9 5
                    ◇ 9 7 5 4 2
                    ♣ K 9 4
  ♠ Q J 6                              ♠ 9 2
  ♡ 8 6 4           ┌─────────┐        ♡ 7 3 2
  ◇ K J             │    N    │        ◇ A 10 6
  ♣ J 10 8 5 2      │ W     E │        ♣ A Q 7 6 3
                    │    S    │
                    └─────────┘
                    ♠ A K 8 7 3
                    ♡ A K Q J 10
                    ◇ Q 8 3
                    ♣ —
```

You play in 4♠ after opening a strong 1♣ in second seat and West leads the jack of clubs. You now see that the hands fit poorly with dummy's sole picture card wasted and its ruffing potential diminished by your solid suit.

West would hardly lead from the ♣A around to a strong hand and you know that East would not pass as dealer with ♣A-Q and ◇A-K. This means that even if you could overcome the entry shortage, there would be no point in playing to your ◇Q.

Two hopes spring to mind: ♠Q-J dropping doubleton and a doubleton ◇A-K, but neither seems likely. Actually, your best chance is to ruff a diamond in dummy! Having ruffed the club, take the bull by the horns and give up a diamond. Fortunately, the defenders cannot untangle the suit and can do no better than play a trump to your ace. You duck a second diamond and ruff the club return. After drawing one more trump, you rattle off the hearts, throwing all dummy's diamonds, and ruff a diamond (or you might ruff the fifth heart and ruff a third club to hand).

Note that you go down if you draw just two rounds of trumps and run the hearts. West will refrain from ruffing and, upon gaining the lead in diamonds, remove dummy's last trump.

Cool Customer

♠ Q 8
♡ Q J 10 5 3
◇ K 8 7 2
♣ J 2

◇ A led

```
    N
 W     E
    S
```

♠ A J 10 9 6 5 4 2
♡ A 2
◇ Q
♣ K 8

Dealer West
Both vul.

WEST	NORTH	EAST	SOUTH
1NT	pass	pass	3♠
pass	4♠	all pass	

In this sequence from the rubber bridge table, West's 1NT is strong, 15-17, and your reopening 3♠ indicates good playing strength but the wrong sort of hand to double.

West, who clearly holds a difficult hand from which to lead, lays down the ace of diamonds. East drops the jack on this and West continues diamonds. How should you plan the play?

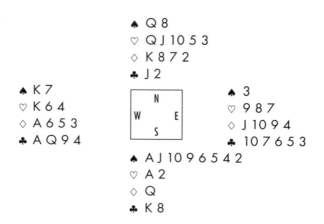

```
              ♠ Q 8
              ♡ Q J 10 5 3
              ◇ K 8 7 2
              ♣ J 2
♠ K 7                        ♠ 3
♡ K 6 4          N          ♡ 9 8 7
◇ A 6 5 3     W     E        ◇ J 10 9 4
♣ A Q 9 4         S          ♣ 10 7 6 5 3
              ♠ A J 10 9 6 5 4 2
              ♡ A 2
              ◇ Q
              ♣ K 8
```

Playing in 4♠, you watch West, who opened a strong notrump, play two rounds of diamonds. Sadly, the bidding tells you that the ♠K, ♡K and ♣A are all offside and that the ♠K will not be singleton. Can you find some good news?

With the missing strength concentrated in one hand, there must be some hope of a throw in, probably after you have squeezed West out of some exit cards. You need to keep the king of clubs guarded until you have driven out the trump king, so you ruff the second diamond in hand. Since the only way to reach the temporarily stranded ◇K is in trumps, you next lead a small trump. West should go in with the king and may as well exit with a trump. You win this in dummy, throw a club on the ◇K, ruff a diamond to hand and run the trumps. To keep ♡K-x, West has to reduce to one club. Therefore, you throw one of dummy's clubs on the last trump and exit with a club to West's now singleton ace.

A cool customer on your left might smoothly blank the ♡K and then throw the ♣Q on the final trump, keeping ♣A-x. If you fall for this, believing that West has a 2-4-4-3 shape, you go down. Thankfully, few opponents defend this well.

Preventative Measures

♠ Q 4 3
♡ Q 4
◇ K Q J 10 7 2
♣ A 10

♡A led

```
      N
  W       E
      S
```

♠ K J 8 7 2
♡ 10 6 3
◇ A 6
♣ Q J 2

Dealer West
E–W vul.

WEST	NORTH	EAST	SOUTH
1♡	2◇	pass	2♠
pass	4♠	all pass	

You are playing that a change of suit response to an overcall creates a one-round force. This method allows you to explore the best fit in many situations and enables you to reserve the cuebid for hands with support for partner.

West leads the ace of hearts (ace from ace-king and others) and continues with the king and five as East follows upwards. How should you proceed from here?

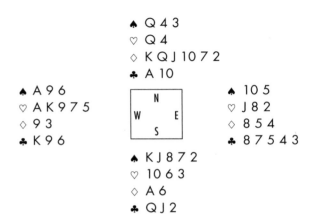

```
                  ♠ Q 4 3
                  ♡ Q 4
                  ◇ K Q J 10 7 2
                  ♣ A 10
    ♠ A 9 6                          ♠ 10 5
    ♡ A K 9 7 5        N             ♡ J 8 2
    ◇ 9 3         W        E         ◇ 8 5 4
    ♣ K 9 6           S             ♣ 8 7 5 4 3
                  ♠ K J 8 7 2
                  ♡ 10 6 3
                  ◇ A 6
                  ♣ Q J 2
```

West, who opened 1♡, starts with three rounds of the suit against your spade game.

With East known to have a third heart, West would hardly underlead the jack, so you ruff the third round low in dummy. You are not worried about the club suit since you plan to lose the lead only once more. In any case, West's failure to switch to a club marks the king onside. Trumps are the problem area.

For two reasons you should cross to the ◇A to play trumps from hand. Firstly, West might have a singleton ace (though you may yet go down). Secondly, you want to avoid a deadly upper-cut on the fourth round of hearts if East has ♠9-x or ♠10-x. Once dummy's queen wins the first trump, you must still take care. If you hastily play a second round, West will win and exit with a diamond to lock you on the table. Before doing so, you must cash a second diamond. This avoids the trump promotion.

You may have noticed that if the second diamond is getting ruffed, you do better not to play it. Of course, West has then erred, as grabbing the first trump and continuing hearts would have defeated the contract. However, if you led the king of diamonds to the ace at Trick 4, you might get a true count signal from East. Did you spot that?

All in Good Time

```
         ♠ 10 9 5
         ♡ J 3
         ◇ A Q 9 7 2
         ♣ A 8 3
```

```
              N
♡ 10 led    W   E
              S
```

```
         ♠ K Q J 8 4 3
         ♡ A 8 6 2
         ◇ 4
         ♣ J 6
```

Dealer East
E–W vul.

WEST	NORTH	EAST	SOUTH
		1♡	1♠
pass	2♡	pass	3♠
pass	4♠	all pass	

As discussed on the previous deal, your partner's cuebid guarantees spade support, normally three cards in length, as well as some values. 6421 types usually play well and you might have jumped all the way to game over this. However, you were concerned about having to deal with several heart losers and the fact that any minor-suit finesses figure to fail.

You cover the ten of hearts with dummy's jack and East plays the queen. Can you see the best line for ten tricks?

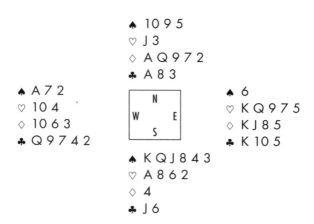

```
              ♠ 10 9 5
              ♡ J 3
              ◇ A Q 9 7 2
              ♣ A 8 3
♠ A 7 2                        ♠ 6
♡ 10 4          N              ♡ K Q 9 7 5
◇ 10 6 3    W      E           ◇ K J 8 5
♣ Q 9 7 4 2        S           ♣ K 10 5
              ♠ K Q J 8 4 3
              ♡ A 8 6 2
              ◇ 4
              ♣ J 6
```

After East opened 1♡, you receive the expected heart lead against your spade game.

To maintain communications (albeit taking the slight risk of a 1-6 heart break) it looks natural to hold off the first heart. Alas, the defenders quickly play two rounds of trumps, killing one of dummy's ruffing winners. With the diamond finesse wrong (as the bidding suggests) and the king well guarded, you cannot set up a second winner in that suit. You end up one down.

Clearly, it will not help to win the first heart trick and return the suit. Again the defenders can remove two of dummy's trumps and you will be left requiring a slice of luck in the diamond suit.

With only one heart ruff available, you must time the play better to benefit from a 4-3 diamond break. Win the first round of hearts, play a diamond to the ace and ruff a diamond; only then give up a heart. As before, the opponents must lead trumps to stop your intended heart ruffs in dummy. You win the second round of trumps in dummy, ruff a diamond and ruff a heart. One more ruff sets up the long diamond and you have the ace of clubs as an entry to it after you have drawn the last trump. This line also caters for ◇K-x with East or, for that matter, with West.

Black Magic

```
        ♠ A 9 8 6 4
        ♡ A 6 5
        ◇ K
        ♣ A Q J 3
```

◇ J led

```
        ┌─────────┐
        │    N    │
        │ W     E │
        │    S    │
        └─────────┘
```

```
        ♠ K J 10 2
        ♡ Q 8 2
        ◇ 5 4
        ♣ 10 9 7 2
```

Dealer East
Both vul.

WEST	NORTH	EAST	SOUTH
		1◇	pass
1♡	dbl	2◇	2♠
3◇	4♠	all pass	

North did the right thing on the first round. With support for both unbid suits and no particular desire for a spade lead, double was much better than a 1♠ overcall.

East captures the singleton king of diamonds with the ace and switches to the nine of hearts. The duplication of distribution leaves you with plenty to do. Can you manage ten tricks?

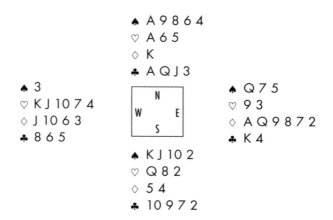

You play in 4♠ after East has bid 1◇ and 2◇, West 1♡ and 3◇. East wins the diamond lead and switches to a heart.

The bidding and early play reveal a lot about the East-West hands. Assuming West has the heart king, East surely has the king of clubs to justify opening, and probably the spade queen as well. Indeed, even if you were unsure of the trump position, you would finesse against East. Do you see why?

With almost the same shape in your two hands and the position of the rounded-suit kings marked, you face four losers in the outside suits: two hearts, one club and one diamond. To cut this number to three you will need to fell the singleton ♣K or achieve an endplay by exiting on the second round to what had been a doubleton king. Either way, you need to find West with length in clubs. Holding presumably six diamonds, two hearts and no more than two clubs, East will have three spades (at least).

Duck the first round of hearts, win the second, draw trumps with the aid of the finesse and ruff a diamond in dummy. Now play ace and another club. East has to concede a ruff and discard on the return and your possible second heart loser vanishes. True, West can overtake the first heart to play a club, but you simply adjust the order of the strip to reach the same ending.

Promised Land

```
              ♠ Q 9
              ♡ K J 10 8 3
              ◇ 10 5 3
              ♣ 6 4 2
```

♣9 led

```
         ┌─────────┐
         │    N    │
         │ W     E │
         │    S    │
         └─────────┘
```

```
              ♠ A 10
              ♡ A 9
              ◇ Q J 7 6
              ♣ A K Q J 3
```

Dealer West
Neither vul.

WEST	NORTH	EAST	SOUTH
3♠	pass	pass	3NT
all pass			

You had a tricky call to make. If partner has the right cards, you might well have a slam in a minor, but 3NT seems a good practical shot. These days a singleton spade will rarely come down in dummy because with three-card spade support East would probably raise the preempt to game.

Presumably fearing that you might hold the ♠A-Q, West leads a club. Where do you go for a ninth trick?

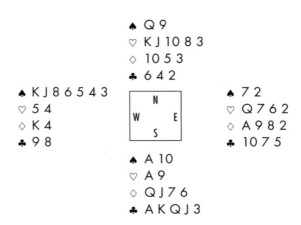

```
              ♠ Q 9
              ♡ K J 10 8 3
              ◇ 10 5 3
              ♣ 6 4 2
♠ K J 8 6 5 4 3        ┌─────────┐        ♠ 7 2
♡ 5 4                  │    N    │        ♡ Q 7 6 2
◇ K 4              W   │         │   E    ◇ A 9 8 2
♣ 9 8                  │    S    │        ♣ 10 7 5
                       └─────────┘
              ♠ A 10
              ♡ A 9
              ◇ Q J 7 6
              ♣ A K Q J 3
```

Playing in 3NT after West has opened 3♠, you receive an unhelp-ful club lead.

You have eight top tricks and various options for a ninth. You could try to develop a diamond trick and wait to see what happens. If West wins the first round, you are confident you can handle a spade switch from that side of the table. Even if East turns up with the king of spades, holding up your ace may well shut West out. There is also a chance, though you would need to read it, that East has both top diamonds (and a presumed double-ton spade). In this case, you could afford to lose the lead twice in diamonds. Alternatively, if, as expected, East wins the first diamond and plays a spade to the king, allowing West to clear the suit, you could fall back on the heart finesse.

Although playing on diamonds does offer some chances, a much stronger line is available, one that should work any time West has the king of spades. Can you see it?

Cash a second club (but not a third — you need an entry), then play ace, king and jack of hearts and throw the spade ace! Whichever way they squirm, the defenders must either give you access to dummy or allow you two diamond tricks.

```
        ♠ 6 3
        ♡ 8 6 5
        ◇ A K 5 3
        ♣ 10 9 3 2

                    ┌─────────┐
                    │    N    │
♡ Q led             │ W     E │
                    │    S    │
                    └─────────┘

        ♠ A K J 10 7 5 4
        ♡ 9 2
        ◇ J 6
        ♣ A K
```

Dealer North
Both vul.

WEST	NORTH	EAST	SOUTH
	pass	2♡	4♠
all pass			

I suppose you would have a slam on if North turned up with queen to three spades, a singleton heart, the ace of diamonds and the queen of clubs. However, it is seldom easy to identify specific cards in partner's hand and one can hardly fault the direct leap to game over East's weak two.

East overtakes the queen of hearts lead with the king and continues with the ace and ten. It looks like you will lose at most two hearts and a trump — is that really true?

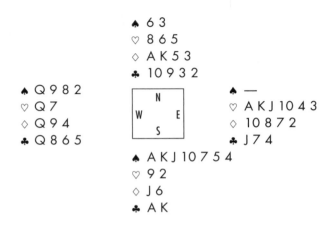

You play in 4♠ after East has shown six hearts and at most 10 points. The defenders play three rounds of hearts.

The danger, obvious enough when you are presented with the deal as a problem, is a 4-0 trump break. If you ruff low, West may overruff and still score another trump trick. If you ruff high, West will discard and have two natural trump tricks.

Well, if you ruff low and West overruffs, retaining ♠Q-9-x, you are bound to lose a second trump; if you ruff very high, you could also lose two trump tricks. However, if you ruff with the jack (or ten), you might lose only one if West has ♠Q-9-8-x and the right shape outside — you will aim to reduce everyone to three cards and then duck a spade. This has to be the plan.

Let us suppose first that West discards a diamond when you ruff the third heart with the jack. Then you cash one top trump, getting the news, unblock the clubs, cross to the ◊A and ruff a club. Next you cross back to the ◊K and ruff a second club. If, instead, West discards a club on the third round of hearts, you start the same way but finish with a diamond ruff.

How do you know which suit to ruff? With 2-5 or 4-3 in the minors, West could beat you by throwing a diamond or a club respectively. So, play for the genuine chance of 3-4.

Dig Deep

```
        ♠ Q 8 7
        ♡ J 10 6 2
        ◊ 9 4
        ♣ A K Q 9
```

```
              N
◊ J led   W       E
              S
```

```
        ♠ A J 4 2
        ♡ Q 9 3
        ◊ A K
        ♣ J 8 6 2
```

Dealer West
Both vul.

WEST	NORTH	EAST	SOUTH
pass	1♣	dbl	redbl
1◊	pass	pass	3NT
all pass			

In the UK, an event involving duplicated boards played at clubs across the country is called a simultaneous pairs. The term has never really caught on in some other parts of the world, I imagine because the presence of several time zones in one nation means that heats take place at different times. North Americans are familiar with the term 'Continent-wide Pairs', for example.

You might have bashed 3NT at your first turn, but it was possible the opponents would do something foolish.

On this deal, you can forget about overtricks despite the scoring method. Can you spot the best way to try for nine?

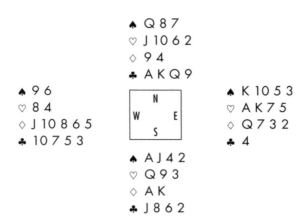

```
              ♠ Q 8 7
              ♡ J 10 6 2
              ◇ 9 4
              ♣ A K Q 9
♠ 9 6                          ♠ K 10 5 3
♡ 8 4          N               ♡ A K 7 5
◇ J 10 8 6 5  W   E            ◇ Q 7 3 2
♣ 10 7 5 3        S            ♣ 4
              ♠ A J 4 2
              ♡ Q 9 3
              ◇ A K
              ♣ J 8 6 2
```

On the awkward but predictable diamond lead, you play in 3NT
after East has doubled North's 1♣ opening and West has bid 1◇
over your redouble.

On the bidding, the chance of a 7-2 diamond break is zero,
which rules out trying to establish the hearts. All will be well if
spades break 3-3, as then straightforward play will give you three
spade tricks. How might you overcome a 4-2 break?

Well, East isn't going to duck the ♠Q when you lead it nor
would he make a minimum takeout double with a doubleton in
an unbid major — the latter tells you that you will not find ♠K-x
onside. West may hold ♠10-9 alone, but can you spot something
better?

If West has ♠9-x or ♠10-x, an intra-finesse will save the day.
After winning the diamond lead perforce, play a spade and cover
the six with the seven, which will lose to East's ten. You win the
next diamond trick, cash two high clubs in dummy and run the
queen of spades. East can cover but the nine drops and you have
the entries to untangle the suit. West does slightly better to play
the nine on the first round, but restricted choice tells you not to
treat this as from 10-9-(x); this is less likely in any event because
East would probably overcall one heart on a 3-5-4-1 shape.

To and Fro

```
        ♠ A 7 3
        ♡ A 8
        ◇ Q 9 6 5 4
        ♣ Q J 10
```

♡ 4 led

```
        ┌─────────┐
        │    N    │
        │ W     E │
        │    S    │
        └─────────┘
```

```
        ♠ K 9 4
        ♡ Q J
        ◇ K 7 3
        ♣ A 9 8 4 3
```

Dealer South
N–S vul.

WEST	NORTH	EAST	SOUTH
			1♣
pass	1◇	pass	1NT
pass	3NT	all pass	

A clairvoyant partner, who knew about your heart holding, might have bashed 3NT in response to your possibly prepared opening bid. Happily, it matters not, as East covers the eight of hearts with the nine and you thankfully win with the queen.

You are still not out of the woods. If things go wrong, the defenders might take three hearts, a club and a diamond. How do you plan to prevent this from happening?

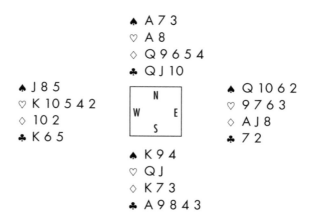

As South, you play in 3NT, having opening 1♣ and rebid 1NT over partner's 1◇ response. West leads the four of hearts to East's nine and your queen.

A successful club finesse would see you home, but you know what to expect in a book of this nature. In any event, 50% represents such a significant chance of failure that you should surely consider alternative lines.

If you can sneak a diamond past the ace (and nobody can afford to go in with it from a two- or three-card holding), you are home. Which opponent should you choose as your victim?

It would be dangerous (mainly because the three and two of hearts are missing) to decide purely on the likelihood that West holds more hearts than East and hence has less room for the missing ace. The bidding provides a much more reliable clue. With the king of clubs, king to five hearts (most likely) and the ace of diamonds, West might very well have overcalled with one heart. So cross over to the spade ace and play a diamond to the king. When this holds, you can afford to lose a club but not to expose the hearts or block the clubs. Therefore, you lead a small club to drive out the king.

Natural Reaction

<pre>
        ♠ A 9 8 5
        ♡ J 2
        ◇ Q J 10 4
        ♣ A 8 2
</pre>

<pre>
              N
♣6 led   W   E
              S
</pre>

<pre>
        ♠ J 10 6 4 3 2
        ♡ K Q 9
        ◇ A
        ♣ 10 5 3
</pre>

Dealer East
E–W vul.

WEST	NORTH	EAST	SOUTH
		pass	1♠
dbl	2NT	pass	3♠
pass	4♠	all pass	

Because a jump raise would signify weakness after West's double, North's 2NT bid indicates a hand with four-card spade support and at least the values to invite game. Holding a bare minimum, you attempt to sign off. Partner has other ideas!

Even if you assume a normal 2-1 trump split, West's club lead poses a grave threat to your contract. How do you hope to avoid losing two clubs, a heart and a trump?

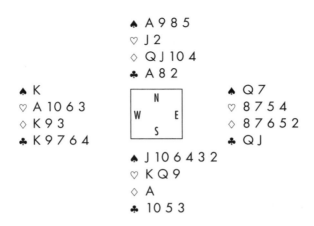

♠ A 9 8 5
♡ J 2
◇ Q J 10 4
♣ A 8 2

♠ K
♡ A 10 6 3
◇ K 9 3
♣ K 9 7 6 4

N
W E
S

♠ Q 7
♡ 8 7 5 4
◇ 8 7 6 5 2
♣ Q J

♠ J 10 6 4 3 2
♡ K Q 9
◇ A
♣ 10 5 3

West, having doubled one spade, leads the ♣6 against your 4♠ contract.

In the absence of any enemy bidding, your natural reaction would be to hope that the player who holds the ace of hearts has a doubleton club and duck the club. Should you still do this?

Give West, say, a 2-3-3-5 shape with three small hearts and 12 points, including ♠K-Q doubleton and ♣K-J-x-x-x (East must have at least one big club or West would lead high). That sounds rather bold for a takeout double, vulnerable against not and facing a passed partner. Besides, what might this leave for East?

The answer is roughly 5-5 in the red suits and 6 points (the ♡A and the ♣Q), a hand that would surely justify bidding 3♡ over 2NT. East might just have the ◇K instead, but you lack the timely entries to take a ruffing finesse and return to dummy.

West would hardly double with two small clubs and surely East would bid 3♣ with K-Q-J-x-x, so there is really only one chance consistent with the bidding and West's low club lead: to find East with K-J or Q-J doubleton in clubs.

To take advantage of this you must put up dummy's ace on the first round to block the suit. You should then cash the ace of spades (in case East has a small singleton trump) and knock out the ♡A. Later you will discard one of dummy's clubs on a heart and ruff a club.

Choice of Evils

```
        ♠ 10 9
        ♡ Q 7 4 3
        ◇ J 10 6
        ♣ A K 10 7
```

◇ K led

```
      ┌─────────┐
      │    N    │
      │ W     E │
      │    S    │
      └─────────┘
```

```
        ♠ A K J 7 6 4 2
        ♡ A 9
        ◇ 2
        ♣ J 9 3
```

Dealer West
Both vul.

WEST	NORTH	EAST	SOUTH
1◇	pass	1♡	1♠
2◇	2♠	pass	4♠
all pass			

Since the opponents play support doubles, West's 2◇ rebid denies holding three hearts. Partner had an awkward bid over this since double would be for penalties and 2NT would indicate a better hand and stronger diamonds.

West leads the ◇K (requesting a count signal) and, on seeing East play the four, switches to the ten of hearts. You win with the ace and decide to cash two top trumps; East follows low once but discards a small heart on the second round. How can you make all but two of the remaining tricks?

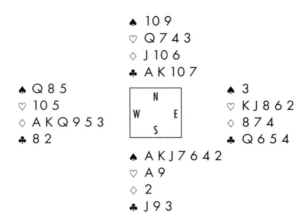

```
                    ♠ 10 9
                    ♡ Q 7 4 3
                    ◇ J 10 6
                    ♣ A K 10 7
♠ Q 8 5                              ♠ 3
♡ 10 5           ┌─────────┐         ♡ K J 8 6 2
◇ A K Q 9 5 3    │ W  N  E │         ◇ 8 7 4
♣ 8 2            │    S    │         ♣ Q 6 5 4
                 └─────────┘
                    ♠ A K J 7 6 4 2
                    ♡ A 9
                    ◇ 2
                    ♣ J 9 3
```

You play in 4♠, West having bid diamonds twice and East hearts once. After West cashes a diamond, you win the heart shift, and two rounds of trumps reveal the 3-1 break, leaving you with a trump loser.

Finding queen to three trumps on your left seems doubly bad news. You know West started with six diamonds and unless hearts are 6-1, East has four clubs, making it 2:1 that the queen sits offside. Can you see a way around this?

You should next concede a trump and pitch a diamond from dummy. Suppose that West switches to a club, won by the ace. In this case, you ruff a diamond to hand and run all the trumps, keeping two clubs and a heart on the table. East, forced to keep the queen of clubs guarded, bares the king of hearts, but you exit with a heart and wait for a club return.

It seems more natural for West to continue hearts when in with the trump queen, but you can handle this as well. The jack wins on your right and, as you hold the club jack, East can do no better than to play a diamond. You ruff and run all but one trump, keeping two hearts and two clubs in dummy. If East saves three clubs and so only one heart, you can ruff out the hearts; if not, the ace and king of clubs will drop the queen to leave your hand high. Well done!

Alternative Route

♠ A 4 3
♡ A 10 8 4
◇ Q 8 7
♣ 10 5 3

♡K led

```
    N
 W     E
    S
```

♠ Q J 10 9 2
♡ 6
◇ A J 5 2
♣ A K 4

Dealer West
E–W vul.

WEST	NORTH	EAST	SOUTH
pass	pass	pass	1♠
dbl	redbl	2♡	pass
pass	2♠	pass	4♠
all pass			

Partner's sequence of actions gives an accurate description: three-card spade support and 10-11 points. You passed over 2♡ to indicate above-minimum values and to find out more. One can construct layouts on which 3NT might prove easier, but 4♠ seems an acceptable contract.

Having captured the king of hearts with dummy's ace, can you see the best route to ten tricks?

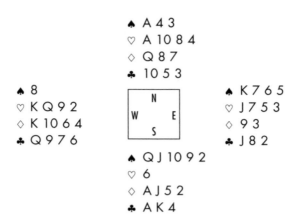

	♠ A 4 3	
	♡ A 10 8 4	
	◇ Q 8 7	
	♣ 10 5 3	

♠ 8		♠ K 7 6 5
♡ K Q 9 2	N	♡ J 7 5 3
◇ K 10 6 4	W E	◇ 9 3
♣ Q 9 7 6	S	♣ J 8 2

	♠ Q J 10 9 2	
	♡ 6	
	◇ A J 5 2	
	♣ A K 4	

You open 1♠ in fourth seat and reach game in the suit after West has made a takeout double and East has bid hearts. You take the opening lead of the king of hearts with the ace.

Entering an auction as a passed hand can be a double-edged sword. Although partner knows your values are limited, you risk giving away vital information if, as happens a fair proportion of the time, you end up defending.

As declarer, you can lay heavy odds on the position of the kings of spades and diamonds. This warns you against the normal line of finessing both suits. Nor does it help to take the diamond finesse and reject the spade finesse. Once the jack of diamonds loses to the king, you are in big trouble because East can ruff the third round of diamonds; you will either lose a club and a second diamond or the equivalent in ruffs.

To succeed you must come over with a club and advance a small diamond. If West grabs the king, dummy's hearts are good enough to protect you from repeated forces — you lose just a spade, a diamond and one other trick. If West prefers to duck, the queen wins and you play two more rounds of the suit, later ruffing your last diamond with dummy's trump ace.

Emergency Exit

♠ Q 8 7 3
♡ J 10 7
◇ A K 10 7 4
♣ 4

♡K led

```
      N
  W       E
      S
```

♠ A 10 5 2
♡ 6 5 3 2
◇ 9 6 3
♣ A Q

Dealer East
E–W vul.

WEST	NORTH	EAST	SOUTH
		1NT	pass
2♠	pass	2NT	pass
3♣	dbl	pass	3♠
all pass			

1NT is strong, 15-17, and 2♠ is a transfer into clubs. East's 2NT announces ♣Q-x-x or better (3♣ would deny support) and North's double of West's signoff seems reasonable, especially at match-point pairs. When dummy appears, you feel very glad about deciding to call your stronger major.

After the ♡K holds, West plays a small heart. East cashes the queen and ace, West throwing a club on the third round. East now switches to the ♣7. It looks like 3♣ would go down, so you need to make your contract. Can you do it?

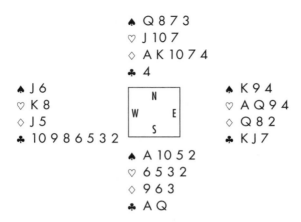

You play in 3♠ after East has announced a strong balanced hand and West a string of clubs. The play starts with three rounds of hearts and a club switch.

A count of points gives good news and bad news. Since West can hold at most two more, the king of clubs must be onside. Unfortunately, the same reasoning makes the double finesse in diamonds hopeless. To avoid a diamond loser you will either need to catch East with ◊Q-J doubleton or arrange a throw-in.

East can hardly hold only two diamonds and two spades, so any endplay must be against West. What might set it up?

You finesse the ♣Q, throw a diamond on the ♣A and cross over with the ◊A. Next, hoping West has ♠J-x, you call for dummy's queen. Whether or not the king covers, you can take a second round of diamonds and lose the next trump to the now singleton jack. Then West must give you a ruff and discard, allowing you to pitch a diamond from hand and crossruff.

This is indeed a tricky contract and my regular partner missed the winning line in the heat of battle. I only spotted the answer some time after I got back home. At any rate, it goes to prove that partscores can provide just as much interest as games.

fateful finesse

♠ A Q
♡ A K 10
◇ A J 10 3
♣ Q J 10 5

```
        N
   W        E
        S
```

♣A led

♠ J 6
♡ Q 6 5 2
◇ K Q 9 8 6 4 2
♣ —

Dealer West
Both vul.

WEST	NORTH	EAST	SOUTH
3♣	3NT	pass	4◇
pass	4♡	pass	5♣
pass	5NT	pass	7◇
all pass			

A 3NT overcall of a preemptive three-bid covers a wide range and 4◇ is clearly forcing (there is no reason to run from a game to a partscore). Four hearts and five clubs are cuebids and 5NT is the grand slam force (Josephine). You exhibit touching faith in partner's bidding at rubber bridge by owning up to two of the top three trumps with your jump to 7◇.

West optimistically leads the ace of clubs. How can you make the most of your chances?

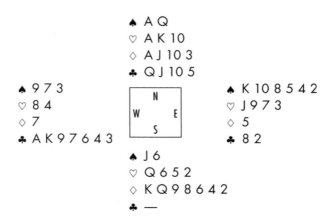

Playing in 7◇ after West has preempted 3♣ in first seat, you receive the ace of clubs lead. You have eleven top tricks, an easy ruff in dummy, and various chances for a thirteenth.

West, having heard you cuebid 5♣, would hardly lead an unsupported ace, which makes the chance of ruffing out the ♣K remote. More practical options include a 3-3 heart break, a short jack of hearts, or a successful spade finesse. Sadly, you can virtually rule out the last of these. With ace-king, king, West would have a very heavy preempt. Indeed, as you can see from the diagram, none of these wishes come true.

The solution is to ruff four clubs in hand. This gives you eight trump winners whilst conserving your squeeze chances if, as seems likely, East has four (or more hearts) and the ♠K. You can draw trumps, cash the ♡A-K (in case the jack falls) and later use the ♠A and two trumps as entries to finish the ruffing and return to dummy. When you lead dummy's fourth trump, you have ♡Q-x (and a spade) in hand and the ♡10 and ♠Q in dummy; East must discard from the ♠K and ♡J-9.